MITSUBISHI A6M1/2/-2N ZERO-SEN

in Japanese Naval Air Service

Richard M. Bueschel

Schiffer Military/Aviation History
Atglen, PA

Cover artwork by Steve Ferguson, Colorado Springs, CO.

NEAR PERFECTION, NEAR BOUGAINVILLE

The nimble Zero-Sen model 22 may well have been the most formidable of all the Zero types. But as of 1943, only the skill of aviators such as Hiroyoshi Hishizawa, Japan's leading fighter pilot of World War II, could compensate for the Zero's obsolescence. Our painting represents Nishizawa and his 251st Group wingmen in yet another dogfight with the superior F4U Corsairs of the U.S. Marines, south of Bougainville during the final campaign for the Solomon Islands as of late 1943.

Hiroyoshi Nishizawa's legendary career began in earnest when he joined the famous Tainan-Lae Wing in April of 1942. After seven months of air battles ranging over Guadalcanal and eastern New Guinea, his score of thirty aerial victories would be the highest of any combatant in the theater. However, combat losses in the Tainan Group as of November forced the ace and his few fellow survivors to withdraw to Japan where they reorganized as the 251st Group. Re-equipped with the upgraded Model 22 Zero, Nishizawa and the 251st returned to Rabaul in May of 1943.

Nishizawa in the Model 22 proved to be near perfection as a weapon. Despite Imperial air units no longer keeping tallies of individual victories after June, newspaper accounts and family memoirs reflect the ace may well have tripled his score as of late October. At that time, the aviator briefly transferred to the 253rd Group, and told his new commander his personal victory tally was eighty-six enemy planes shot down.

In November of 1943, Nishizawa returned home and remained there for a year, both as an instructor and as a home defense pilot over northern Honshu. While there he made no contact with the enemy. With the invasion of the Philippine Islands in October of 1944, Nishizawa entered into his third tour and advanced to Luzon where he flew one interception of U.S. Navy Hellcats over Clark Field on the 25th to claim two final victories. After diverting to Cebu Island, the ace took a transport flight back to Luzon the following day, only to fall victim enroute to another Hellcat raid. The leading ace of the Pacific war was dead at the age of twenty-four. His epic achievements garnered him the sacred heroic name, Bukai-in Kohan Giko Kyoshi, a posthumous title of the most noble honors in Zen-Buddhism.

This title was originally published by Osprey Publications Ltd. in 1970.

Book Design by Mary Jane MJ Hannigan

Library of Congress Catalog Number: 95-67278

Printed in the United States of America.
ISBN: 0-88740-754-4

Published by Schiffer Publishing Ltd.
77 Lower Valley Road
Atglen, PA 19310
Please write for a free catalog.
This book may be purchased from the publisher.
Please include $2.95 postage.
Try your bookstore first.

We are interested in hearing from authors with book ideas on related topics.

Nakajima production of the Mitsubishi-designed A6M2 began a month before Pearl Harbor. Nakajima ultimately produced 6,215 Reisen fighters of various models, about two-thirds of the total A6M production. Nakajima G5N1 Shinzan bomber prototype, based on the American Douglas DC-4 sold to Japan, is in the immediate background. Courtesy Dr. Hidemusa Kimura.

MITSUBISHI A6M1/2/-2N ZERO-SEN

It was late in the afternoon on June 4, 1942 when Lieutenant Colonel Sweeney of the United States Army Air Corps decided to throw his four remaining B-17E Flying Fortress bombers into the battle for Midway. An hour later two more patched up Fortresses took off from the Midway island airfield. There wasn't much else left after the earlier Japanese carrier plane attacks. The American advantage in the battle, a code-breaking intelligence coup that revealed the Japanese plans, was of little consequence when it came to the sheer weight of equipment that the Japanese were able to place on the scene. The Americans were out-gunned, outnumbered and out-manned. Reports came through that four large Japanese Fleet carriers had been hit during the day, and were presumed lost. But nobody was sure. Sweeney's Fortresses went looking for the Imperial Fleet, found some surface elements and then fought for their lives as they were jumped by a flock of the deadly "Zero Fighters." The battle was obviously far from over. The Japanese appeared to have victory within their grasp, for it was apparent that the loss of the carriers Soryu, Kaga, Akagi and Hiryu hadn't stopped the intrusive assault on Midway for control of the Central Pacific. The "Zeros" in the air proved that. There was apparently one, or perhaps even more, Fleet carriers in the vicinity. As the night of June 4 moved into the dawn of June 5, the small garrison at Midway braced for the inevitable invasion.

It never came. As Sweeney's B-17's left the waters temporarily under enemy control, the Japanese Mitsubishi-designed and often Nakajima-built A6M2 Type 0 Ship-Based (Carrier) Fighters sputtered out their last drops of usable fuel, and pancacked into the sea. They were from the carrier Hiryu, the last Japanese carrier to be hit by the American SBD Dauntless dive bombers that fateful afternoon, and

Crewmen ready to release the chocks prior to launching the First Attack Wave of fighters under command of Lieut. Commander Itaya of the carrier Akagi. Pearl Harbor Attack, December 8 (Japanese time) 1941. Courtesy Shorzoe Abe.

had no place to land. An alarming inventory of the finest carrier combat planes ever to put to sea in their time bubbled to the bottom of the Pacific, taking the Japanese plans for territorial expansion by force of arms with them. No Japanese fighter plane ever flew this close to the American heartland again. The greatest naval battle since Trafalgar ended with an American victory of magnificent proportions, but the United States didn't realize it for a full day. In just less than six months since the Pearl Harbor attack of December 7, 1941 (American time), the Japanese thrust, spearheaded across its broad fronts by the Zero-Sen (in translation called the same thing by the Pacific Allies – "Zero-Fighter"), had been blunted. It would take another three years of bloody fighting before it would all be over, but after Midway the issue was never in doubt. Japan, and the Zero-Sen, had a brief moment of great glory, followed by a long, grinding path of retribution. This is the story of that journey, and of what is regarded as the best-known single aircraft of the Pacific War.

Creation of a myth

By the middle 1930s American-trained Mitsubishi engineer Jiro Horikoshi had created the uniquely Japanese 9-Shi fighter, which ultimately reached production as the A5M1 Type 96 Ship-Based (Carrier) Fighter, entering unit service in numbers in models up to the A5M4 in the late 1930s. Not one to let a technological advantage lapse, the Japanese Naval Air Force (JNAF) called for a replacement in May 1937, and Jiro Horikoshi's staff undertook the design of the 12-Shi fighter. By October the original JNAF specifications were tightened up, based on combat experience in China. Originally in competition with Nakajima for the production order, Horikoshi's experience and Nakajima's reluctance to lose money on the changing project left Mitsubishi alone in the field by the end of January 1938. By April the basic design was approved by the Naval Aeronautical Establishment at Yokosuka, and by the summer of 1938 Mitsubishi was cutting metal to build the prototype. Under Horikoshi's guidance, structure engineers Yoshitoshi Sone and Yoshio Yoshikawa made liberal use of the newly created ESD Extra Super-Duralumin to lighten the airframe. Other technical tricks were applied to keep the aircraft light and enhance its fighting maneuverability. Interconnecting structures, with the wing spar an integral part of both wing and fuselage, reduced individual assemblies while cradling the two wing cannon. This alone saved over a hundred pounds weight of fasteners and connectors. The heavy safety devices gaining growing acceptance in Europe and America, such as pilot armour and self-sealing fuel tanks, were

Over a year before the Pearl Harbor Attack the Type 0 Ship-Based (Carrier) Fighter was flying combat missions over China. These are 12-Shi prototypes, later designated A6M2 Model 11, during evaluation trials prior to assignment in China. Sekai no Kokuki.

ignored in the weight-saving engineering. Lightweight plywood auxiliary fuel tanks were even added as a lash-on to increase the range greatly without adding the weight of additional airframe tankage. The resulting completely original fighter design weighed less than any comparable fighter in the world while carrying the heavy specified armament of two 20mm cannons and two 7.7mm machine guns, and quickly found acceptance in the JNAF in a form that would have been thoroughly unacceptable in the other major aircraft carrier using nations such as Britain, France or the United States.

This stress on maneuverability at the expense of strength and safety did not cause problems for years to come, for in the hands of good pilots the Allied enemy never really had a chance to get a shot at the high-performing Zero-Sen. But ultimately the cost was high, both in production and in combat. The basic structure was a complicated single-unit assembly and took a long time to produce per piece. It was impossible to build major Zero-Sen components in a variety of plants for assembly at a collecting point. With more A6M fighters produced between 1940 and August 1945 than any other Japanese aircraft type – the excessive production time added up to a loss of productive capability. In combat, once the Allied pilots caught on to the weaknesses of the Zero-Sen and learned that it would virtually crumble or blow up under heavy machine gun or cannon fire, the losses of the Zero-Sen rapidly climbed past the point of acceptability, until even its own pilots would rather avoid a fight than chance their destruction. But all of that was well in the future, and only a pundit could have guessed that the engineering marvel presented to the JNAF as the completed 12-Shi Ship-Based Fighter could provide the Imperial Navy with anything but power and fame.

The A6M2 Model 11 Reisen entered combat evaluation in August 1940 in China. This is aircraft No. 177 of the 12th Combined Group stationed at Hankow, China, in September 1940. Fuselage band denotes Section Leader.Courtesy Seiso Tachibana.

Model 11 Reisen No. 163 of the 12th Combined Group over Hankow, China, late 1940. Sekai no Kokuki.

The first prototype, receiving the designation A6M1, was completed in February 1939 at Mitsubishi's experimental shops at Nagoya. On March 19 it was wheeled under wraps by ox cart to the Japanese Army Air Force (JAAF) field at nearby Kagamigahara where it flew on the afternoon of April 1 piloted by civilian Katsuzo Shima, a Mitsubishi test pilot. On April 25 Shima got the aircraft barely over 300 m.p.h. and fell just short of the original JNAF specs for a speed of 312 m.p.h. Naval pilots

Kept secret for well over a year of combat service, this first "public" photograph of the A6M2 was released to the Japanese press immediately after the Pearl Harbor Attack. All revealing markings have been retouched out of the picture. Koku Asahi.

Out with the old! In with the new! Mitsubishi 96 Kansen A5M4 Type 96 Ship-Based (Carrier) Fighters fly overhead as the new A6M2 is readied for service, November 1941. Koku Asahi.

began to fly the A6M1 in July. No major design faults showed up, and a vibration harmonic was eliminated by using a constant speed 3-bladed airscrew in place of the original variable pitch 2-blader. The only real problem seemed to be speed and the inability of the 780 h.p. Mitsubishi Zuisei 13 engine to put it over the top. While a second A6M1 prototype was being completed the JNAF gave the go-ahead to a more powerful model as the A6M2 powered by the 940 h.p. Nakajima Sakae 12 of 940 h.p. It became the classic "Zero-Fighter" production model and, with little basic change from its prototype, flew in this form until the end of the Pacific War.

With naval acceptance of the A6M1 on September 14, 1939 after 162 hours of flying time, secret carrier trials began. The A6M1 didn't pass, and for a while it looked as if the whole 12-Shi program was stalled. Then, when the second A6M1 prototype, flown for the first time in October, blew up in mid-air on March 11, 1940, killing its naval pilot, an engineering examination was demanded. A redesign of the wing, and strengthened spars, further improved the budding A6M2. With the first A6M2 12-Shi completed in December 1939, followed by an additional A6M2 in early l940, the design was finalizing.

By December 8, 1941 the Model 21 was available in unit strength, with over 400 Zero-Sen fighters delivered to the JNAF prior to the Pearl Harbor Attack. Koku Asahi.

The new prototype took to the air on January 18,1940. While trials with this, and the second prototype, were underway the Imperial Navy decided to jump the developmental and combat evaluation time and ordered an additional 15 prototypes for operational testing in China. Work was rushed, briefly held up after the March 11 explosion, and pushed again. Originally scheduled to be sent to China in May, in spite of delays the aircraft were ready at the end of June. By the first week in July a cadre of select A5M4 96 Kansen pilots were being converted to the experimental A6M2, flying in two new JNAF squadrons of the12th Combined Naval Air Group in China, created for the purpose. Carrier trials also took place at sea on the Kaga in June, and this time the faster, more powerful A6M2 was obviously passing with glory. The Japanese Navy had a remarkable new contemporary fighter ready for production less than a year after World War II began in Europe. The seeds for surprise were sown.

Saburo Sakai's Zero-Sen 3-183 of the 12th Combined Group over China in the summer of 1941. Sekai no Kokuki.

Introduction to combat

No fighter aircraft type ever entered combat receiving more care and attention than the first group of Mitsubishi 12-Shi A6M2 pre-production prototypes. Hand made, radically new and each one literally a research project, the dozen or so aircraft left for Hankow, China, overseas home of the 12th Group, on July 21, 1940, under the care of Lieutenant Tamotsu Yokoyama and Lieutenant Saburo

Shindo, their two youthful squadron commanders. Just as they were setting up in China the final reports of the preliminary testing on the Kaga as well as the Yokosuka Naval Air Test Center were completed, and Mitsubishi's new fighter was accepted for JNAF production on July 31, 1940 as the A6M2 Type 0 Ship-Based (Carrier) Fighter, Model 11. It immediately became the Reisen, or "Zero-Fighter", although the Japanese themselves preferred the Anglicized version and more often called it the Zero-Sen.

Production plans moved quickly, with production-model A6M2's being built at Mitsubishi's No. 3 Airframe Works at Nagoya the first week in August, with finished aircraft rushed to China to join the led to the deletion of the aileron compensation trim tabs with production aircraft No. 127.

With all of these changes accomplished the design was frozen and arrangements were made to have the A6M2 Model 21 produced by Nakajima also, with the first production model coming off the lines at Koizumi late in November I941. Experience in China, and on the carriers, improved the breed so completely that the ultimate production model was virtually de-bugged in less than a year after the first pre-production prototypes took to the air in combat over Hankow, China in August I940, a remarkable rate of value-analysis at a time when such sophisticated engineering was in its infancy.

The experience in China with the experimental

Stiff-winged A6M2 Model 11 Zero-Sen flown by Saburo Sakai over China, 1941. Sakai survived the Pacific War to be the Japanese Navy's leading living Ace. Sekai no Kokuki.

hand-crafted 12-Shi combat prototypes. By the end of November almost fifty had been built with modifications incorporated during production based on the hundreds of flying hours stacking up in the evaluation flights in China. The main spar was strengthened after September, and by late November the airframe was modified to manually fold the wingtips to enable the Reisen to fit standard Fleet Carrier elevators. With this change the A6M2 became the Model 21, remaining in production in this form for over two years. Vibration problems, and the death of a Yokosuka test pilot on April 17, 1941, A6M2 models, soon joined by production A6M2 Model 11's, was successful beyond the wildest dreams of the JNAF planners. By the summer of 1940 the war had moved so far inland that the Imperial Navy's heaviest G3M2 bombers had to attack a well-defended Chungking without fighter escort due to the long ranges. Arrival of the Reisens changed the picture completely. Flying missions of over 1,000 miles round-trip Lieutenant Yokoyama led his squadron of 12-Shi fighters over Chungking on an escort mission on August 19, I940 with Lieutenant Shindo following with his squadron the next

Fighters on the deck of the carrier Akagi as the Nagumo Force crossed the Western Pacific on its way to Pearl Harbor. Hiko Nippon.

day. The defending Chinese fighters oddly remained out of sight and the disappointed Japanese pilots returned to their base without the taste of battle. The earlier Chinese tactics had consisted of diving passes at sitting-duck bombers. With the arrival of the new Japanese fighters, the Chinese held back and avoided combat.

It wasn't until almost a month later, on September 13, that the Zero-Sen drew first blood. Pretend-

En-route to Hawaii the aircrews were informed that their target was the American naval base at Pearl Harbor. Asahigraph.

ing to leave the target area with the bombers, the Japanese fighters under command of Lieutenant Saburo Shindo and Sub-Lieutenant Ayao Shirane suddenly turned around and came back over Chunking about thirty minutes later. Diving out of the sun into a sky crowded with Chinese fighters, the Japanese shot down 27 Polikarpov I-15s, I-16s, and Curtiss Hawk III fighters in half-an-hour. The first Zero-Sen "ace" came out of this single battle, when Petty Officer Koshiro Yamashita shot down five of the Russian-built Chinese fighters. Yamashita later went on to become one of the ranking JNAF aces of the Pacific War with a confirmed score of nine kills and an unofficial rating of over ten. The 12th Combined Air Group fighters had gained a major victory without loss to themselves.

Then combat got sparse again, and Chinese aircraft stayed out of their way. Ranging deep into China, the Japanese fighters gained proficiency and searched vainly for targets. Psychologically the Japanese felt invincible, and their frustration at

The early morning hours of Sunday, December 7 (Hawaiian time), 1941, while America slept. Pilots of the 1st Carrier Division man their planes on the high seas. Shashin Shuho.

being unable to engage in aerial combat made itself shown in various ways. In a raid against Chengtu on October 4, four of the Japanese Zero-Sens in a flight led by Superior Petty Officer Ichiro Higashiyama actually landed on the Chinese airfield and the pilots attempted to blow up the aircraft while their A6M2's sat at the edge of the field with their engines ticking over. The fantastic audacity of the Japanese carried them through, and in spite of a withering ground fire they damaged some aircraft and got away while their comrades in the air pinned

On the alert for the Pearl Harbor Attack. Ground crewmen ready to release on signal. Koku Asahi.

Preparing for battle on the carrier Akagi. The Japanese expected counterattacks from Hawaii and flew Zero-Sen CAP missions over their carriers all day on December 8 (Japanese time). The attacks never came. Courtesy Richard L. Seely.

the defenders down with a constant series of strafing runs. In the heat of action the stupidity of the move was ignored. Had only one of the pilots received a minor wound, or been killed, the Chinese at Chengtu would have been left with a newly-produced Zero-Sen prototype. Conveniently, Chengtu was also the main experimental and aircraft evaluation base of the Chinese Air Force.

Perhaps the most disappointed man of all was Claire Lee Chennault, an American adviser to Chinese leader Chiang Kai-Shek, and commander of the Chinese Air Force. Chennault had been collecting data on the Zero-Sen since its first appearance over Chungking late in August, and was vainly trying to learn its secrets to develop counter-tactics. With the Chengtu opportunity missed, all he could do was watch helplessly as the months rolled by and his demoralized Chinese pilots fell one by one before the guns and cannon of the A6M2. The commando-like raid on Chengtu also had a profound effect on the Chinese, generating a defeatist attitude that further cut the efficiency of the Chinese Air Force. When Zero-Sens and A5M4 96 Kansen fighters of a detached unit of the 12th Combined Air Group began to raid the Chinese training base at Kunming from the new Japanese airfields in occupied French Indo-China in October, the spirit of the Chinese Air Force was broken, and the Japanese gained full command of the air over central and southern China. By the end of 1940 the JNAF had used somewhat over a hundred 12-Shi, Model 11 and Model 21 Zero-Sens ever China and reportedly shot down 59 Chinese aircraft while destroying 101 others. Throughout the fighting not a single Zero-Sen fighter was lost.

As the fighting tapered down in China, the Zero-Sen still held its record of superiority over its foe. Virtually alone in Chinese skies throughout 1941 while the JNAF reorganized its forces to be prepared in the event of a Pacific War, the Zero-Sens reportedly shot down an additional 45 Chinese planes while destroying or damaging 62 others on the ground by the end of September 1941. In one raid on Chengtu on March 14, they shot down 24 Chinese aircraft plus three probables. A raid on Chengtu by JNAF heavy bombers on May 20 was escorted by thirty A6M2's. It was during this raid that the first Zero-Sen was lost in combat, with Superior Petty Officer Kimura's A6M2 crashing as a result of ground fire. By September, only one other A6M2 had been lost, also to ground fire. Thousands of miles away from their home, the Japanese owned the skies over China.

It seemed that only a miracle could ever shoot a Japanese aircraft down in China again – but even that was created by the Zero-Sens. To combat the malaise that had taken hold in the Chinese Air Force after the attack on Chengtu in October 1940, Generalissimo Chiang Kai-Shek called in Chennault and proposed the idea of a mercenary force of American pilots flying modern American planes in the defense of China. The idea took hold, aircraft were made available, and the American Volunteer Group (A.V.G.) "Flying Tigers" was formed. In a little over a year the A.V.G. was demonstrating the combat deficiencies of the Reisen in Chinese skies.

In Fleet Service

As the Zero-Sen made its backwards introduction into service as a land fighter, the weapons system that would conquer more global mass in six months than any military force in history was being developed: the A6M2 Model 21 and the Fleet Carrier. At the time the A6M2 was accepted for production as a carrier fighter in the summer of 1940, following successful trials on the Kaga, the Imperial Navy had only four large Fleet Carriers, with numerous other light and training carriers. By April 1941 Zero-Sen contingents had been formed on the carriers Kaga, Akagi, Hiryu and Soryu. By the summer of 1942 two additional large carriers had joined the fleet, with the folding wingtips of the Model 21 permitting use of the aircraft on every fighting carrier in the Imperial Navy.

One day away from Hawaii the Imperial Navy's battle flag is raised. A Zero-Sen stands on the flight deck of the Akagi. Courtesy Richard L. Seely.

Reisens warming up on the deck of the Akagi the morning of December 8th, Japanese time, prior to launching for the Pearl Harbor Attack. Courtesy M. Toda.

Sheltered from combat, but given almost a year to gain proficiency with their aircraft and home carriers, the rigidly trained Japanese carrier fighter pilots gained confidence. There was reason for this optimism. American and British carriers were still flying biplanes, while their launch and recovery timing was slow, according to reports from Lieutenant Commander Minoru Genda, the Navy's Assistant Naval Air Attache in London. Genda was himself a former 96 Kansen fighter pilot with combat experience in China. He had a philosophy of tactical fighter application similar to Chennault's in China, that of massed fighter use over combat areas to gain total air control, thereby permitting bombing or other air, sea or ground actions with impunity.

Genda's two years in London, and his return to Japan in 1941 during the carrier conversions when A6M2 fighters replaced the open-cockpit and fixed-gear A5M4, had a profound effect on the first combat use of the carrier-based A6M2 and the coming of the Pacific War. When the daring plan to attack Pearl Harbor, conceived in January 1941 by Admiral Isoroku Yamamoto, C-in-C of the Imperial Navy, was first laid out before Rear Admiral Takijiro Onishi, Chief of Staff of the 11th Air Fleet, Onishi asked Genda's opinion. Genda studied the concept in detail, and provided Onishi with a lengthy report on the feasibility of the attack, stressing the use of all six fleet carriers, competent commanders and experienced pilots. By the summer of 1941 the attack plans moved from the feasible to the actual, and Zero-Sen carrier training was increased.

Waiting for the moment of release for the Reisens on the deck of the Akagi. Courtesy Richard L. Seely.

Following the commissioning of the carriers Shokaku and Zuikaku in August 1941, the first elements of Zero-Sens were already flying from their decks in September. Combat trained pilots from the 12th Combined Air Group flying Model 21s in China were brought back to Japan and reassigned to the carriers on account of their invaluable experience. Lieutenant Ayao Shirane was assigned to the Zuikaku. Lieutenant Fusata Iida, an "ace" with 7 kills, went to the Soryu. Lieutenant Commander Shigeru Itaya, also an "ace", became the fighter commander of the Akagi. Now a Commander, Minoru Genda became the Operations Officer to Vice-Admiral Chuichi Naguma and was assigned to the 1st Air Fleet on the Akagi, the flagship of the Pearl Harbor attack force. It was during the first week in November 1941 in the weapons room of

The signal is given. Release on the carrier Shokaku. Shashin Shuho.

An Akagi fighter, one of nine, takes off in the First Wave against Hawaii. Courtesy Richard L. Seely.

The first Reisen launched against Pearl Harbor claws into the air from the carrier Akagi. Courtesy Richard L. Seely.

the carrier, that Genda first unveiled a scale model of Pearl Harbor and began to go over the specific details of the forthcoming attack with the commanders of the various aircraft elements assigned to the six carriers.

While the carrier forces were being trained for their waterbased mission, a number of land-based Groups of the JNAF also began to receive the A6M2 in numbers. With the prime military objectives of war in the Pacific the oil and raw materials of the Dutch Indies, reached by way of the Philippines and Malaya, arrangements were made for attacks to coincide with the raid on Hawaii. In a plan so ambitious it almost defies belief, re-equipping and training for simultaneous attacks on all fronts got underway in the fall of 1941.

1st Class Petty Officer Teimei Akamatsu, third ranking Japanese fighter pilot "ace" in China, got his first chance to fly the Zero-Sen in October 1941. Akamatsu had been assigned to the 3rd Group at Kanoya, where the unit was in training for the assault on the Philippines. The plan was to stretch the range of the A6M2 so that the Philippines attack could be made in a single flight from Formosa, thus avoiding the need for carriers which could then be released for the Pearl Harbor attack. Petty Officer Saburo Sakai, who was destined to survive the war as the JNAF's third ranking "ace", received the same training in the Taman Group located at Tainan, on Formosa. Other units, including the Genzan and Kanoya Groups, destined to open the war from Indo-China; the Ominato, Omura and Yokosuka Groups combining combat readiness and training; and the Kasumigaura and Oita Groups as training bases, received the A6M2 prior to Pearl Harbor, although their numbers were spread extremely thin as less than 400 ultimately reached service before December 8, 1941 (Japanese time), the last day of official peace in the Far East.

Taking off from the deck of the carrier Shokaku on the way to the opening battle in the Pacific War. Courtesy Richard L. Seely.

The cameraman's hand shakes under the tension and the pounding of the seas. Sekai no Kokuki.

Beginning to move on the Akagi. Courtesy Noboru Jyoko.

The "Big War" Begins

Coursing across the Pacific in heavy seas, the attacking Nagumo Force heading for Hawaii in the first days of December 1941 carried with it the largest force of experienced combat pilots outside Europe. On December 2, 1941 Captain Jisaku Okada, Commander of the Kaga, told the crew of his carrier that their mission was to attack Pearl Harbor. The whole of the Imperial Navy's "Outer Combat Force" was committed to the operation. The plan was to attack Hawaii, and then hit Wake Island on the return trip; this was to be followed by attacks in the South Seas.

The Japanese struck at dawn, with Lieut. Commander Shigeru Itaya of the Akagi the fighter Strike Commander in charge of the 45 Zero-Sens from all six carriers in the First Attack Wave. Already an "ace" in China, Itaya led over Hawaii a group of pilots who were equally skilled in combat. Lieutenant Masaharu Suganami, a veteran carrier pilot, led

One by one the first aircraft to attack American soil launch, assemble and head for Hawaii in waves. Hiko Nippon.

The performance of the A6M2 was so superior to its opponents that it served equally well and a land- or ship-based air superiority fighter. Sora.

the Soryu fighters in the First Attack Wave, and remained over the target area to watch for the arrival of the Second Attack Wave. When he finally returned to the Soryu, only a few drops of fuel were left.

The Second Attack Wave was led by Lieutenant Shindo of the Akagi, in charge of a group of 36 Zero-Sen fighters from the Akagi, Kaga, Soryu and Hiryu. A total of 81 A6M2 fighters were sent to Hawaii that Sunday morning, with an additional 54 flying Combat Air Patrol (CAP) over the six carriers in a series of three patrols of 18 aircraft each. The fighters sent to Hawaii had the mission of strafing and destroying American Army and Navy fighter aircraft on the ground and in the air. Then, once the skies were cleared, they were to strafe and generate confusion. They became recognized as the most fearful weapon used at Pearl Harbor as

Newly delivered A6M2 Model 21 prior to assignment to the Zuikaku, early 1942. Kokutishiki.

The first "Zero Fighter" shot down by the Americans at Pearl Harbor was an A6M2 downed at Fort Kamehameha. It was displayed in the hangar to reveal its secrets. Aircraft is AI-154 from the Akagi flown by Class Petty Officer Takeshi Hirano. USAAF.

their slashing attacks hit a broader range of targets and affected more people, both military and civilian, than any other aircraft types in the raid. While the JNAF planners based their calculations on a 50% loss of aircraft over Hawaii, by actual count only nine Zero-Sens were lost- three in the First Wave and six in the Second. While the losses were certainly modest, and less than planned, it was recognized that over four times as many Zero-Sens were lost in a single raid over American territory than were lost in China in well over a year. The Zero-Sen was the victor, but there were signs that the going was getting tougher.

Most of the Zero-Sen wreckage at Hawaii was mangled beyond recognition, or lost in the bay, but the first A6M2 to be downed by American forces was still in visible form, although sliced in half. This was AI-154 from the Akagi, flown by 1st Class Petty Officer Takeshi Hirano. Intact enough for preliminary study, the new fighter greatly impressed the American technical experts assigned to its dissection. Why the United States should have been surprised by the Zero-Sen at Hawaii is one of the mysteries of the Pacific War. Warnings had repeatedly been sent to Washington since the appearance of the fighter in China the previous year. Chennault even had drawings and rough (although a little too optimistic) performance data prepared, and French observers watching the JNAF units in occupied Indo-China in mid-1941 sent back sketches and data. A preliminary recognition manual under preparation by the USAAF in November 1941 had a reasonable representation of the A6M2 on its pages, but release was delayed for many months. The fact remains that the "Zero Fighter" came as a complete surprise to the American combat forces trained to expect an antiquated biplane air force in the event of trouble with Japan.

After Pearl Harbor, fear of the "Zero" raced through the American and Allied air forces. The Japanese fighter was credited with performance and maneuverability far beyond its ability. For the Americans, long conditioned to the words "Made In Japan" meaning an inferior and often copy-cat product, the thought that a Japanese aircraft was in any way superior to American aircraft was too much to comprehend. Authoritative sources soon claimed that the "Zero" was originally an American design, rejected in the United States then purchased, copied and reproduced in Japan. This fiction was so widely circulated that many Allied veterans of the Pacific War still believed that it was true many years after the war. Other sources variously claimed that the "Zero" was copied from the

Vultee Vanguard, the Chance-Vought V.143, the Northrop FT-I, and the Gloster F. 5/34 experimental fighter. The suggestion that the maneuverable Japanese fighter was made of light weight plywood and plastics, a far-reaching technological achievement beyond the design capability of Western nations, even gained acceptance for a short period. With myths replacing facts, the search was on for an intact Zero-Sen for evaluation and information. The scant wreckage at Hawaii, and the lack of available examples for months to come, made the aircraft the most sought-after technological prize of the early months of the Pacific War.

Master of the Skies

Later in the day after the attack at Hawaii, and long hours after the initial planned assault due to poor weather, Zero-Sens appeared over the Philippines. In spite of the warning provided American forces by radio from Hawaii, virtually the entire strength of the American and Philippine air forces were lined up on their airfields. When the 84 Zero-Sens of the 3rd and Tainan Groups, flying from their Southern Formosan bases at Tainan, Takao, Taichu and Palau, first arrived over their targets at Clark and Nichols Field and Iba Field on the west coast of Luzon, they suddenly felt the long over-water trip was worth the effort. They had surprised the defending air forces during lunchtime, and in one day American air power in the Philippines was cut back beyond the point of usefulness. By the end of December Zero-Sens were operating out of bases at Davao and Jolo in the Philippines, to remain until the islands were completely conquered.

The next few weeks saw a surge of activity in which victory followed victory so repeatedly that the Japanese began to feel that it was their destiny to rule the East-Asian and Western Pacific world. The acclaimed hero of the victory was the Zero-Sen, reported in the press, on hand at every action, and reportedly invincible in the air. The 1st Carrier Division coming back from Hawaii, struck at Wake Island. A determined defense led to assignment of the Soryu and Hiryu to a repeat attack by Zero-Sen fighters on December 20. Splitting up at Wake, the Akagi, Kaga, Zuikaku and Shokaku were by January 20, 1942, attacking sleepy Rabaul, an Australian base in New Britain. By the next day this fleet was making aerial strikes with A6M2 fighters at Lae, Salamaua and Madang on the east coast

Tantalizingly little remnants of the apparently invincible "Zero" were recovered in the early months of the war. This example from the carrier Hiryu was shot down over Port Darwin, Australia, in the first raid on February 19, 1942. USAAF.

The feared "Zero Fighter," as it came to be known, was literally everywhere as the Japanese Navy carriers and land based units ranged across the Southwest Pacific and moved down the Dutch Indies. Sora.

of New Guinea. On January 31, nine Zero-Sens flying from Truk, the Japanese strong point in the Western Pacific, landed at Vunakanau Airfield on Rabaul and the build-up of this keystone Japanese base began.

While the carrier forces extended the arm of expansion in long strokes, the land-based Groups of the JNAF moved across the land bridge of the Dutch Indies to reach the same goals. After the Philippine operations, the Zero-Sen units were joined by the Genzan and Kanoya Groups from Malaya and Indo-China, becoming the East Indies force for the final drive through Java. It was during this move that the Tainan Group became the unit with the greatest number of "aces" in the JNAF. Chinese veterans like Petty Officers Kuniyoshi Tanaka, Saburo Sakai, and Tainan Group Commander Lieutenant Junichi Sasai were joined by newcomers Toshio Ota, Torakichi Takatsuka, Hiroyoshi Nishizawa and others. Tanaka had shot down twelve aircraft in China and added eight more kills as the Tainan Group worked its way to its advance base at Lae, New Guinea. Nishizawa went on to become the leading JNAF "ace" of the war.

Other units were rapidly formed and sent into the war zones as additional Zero-Sen production became available. When the Pacific War began the Imperial Navy had 660 fighters, of which half were A6M2 Model 21's By the end of March 1942 some 300 fighters had been lost in combat patrol and training while an additional 316 were delivered to the Navy. Most of the new fighters were Zero-Sens, and units were re-equipped and formed with the fighter. The 1st, 6th and Chitose Group were assigned to the Japanese Mandate Islands in the "Inner South Seas," with Chitose fighters at newly-

A rare prize in an almost intact A6M2 Model 21 of the Tainan Group operating out of Lae, New Guinea, and shot down in a raid over Port Moresby, July 1942. USAAF.

In the early months of the war, Hokoku (Patriotism) aircraft donated to the Imperial Navy by public subscription were boldly marked on the sides of the fuselage. Koku Asahi.

The land based A6M2 Model 21 fighters of the 3rd Group cut a swatch across the South Pacific in 1942. Courtesy Seiso Tachibana.

won Wake Island and others at Aur, Kwajalein, Marus, Wotje and other islands in the chains. As Rabaul was enlarged, elements of the Genzan, Tainan 4th and 6th Groups flying the A6M2 formed the station defense and offense units. The Hyakuri, Saeki and Yatabe Groups received Zero-Sens as training units in Japan, while the 3rd, which later became the 202nd, moved through the Indies to the Celebes and finally Timor in the "North of Australia" combat theater. The Takao Air Group was added to the area to fly convoy escort and provide air cover over Western New Guinea and Northern Australia.

The most active elements of the JNAF remained the carrier forces, with the fighters of the 1st Air Fleet striking across thousands of miles of water. "Navy Naughts", as the Australians sometimes called the Zero-Sen, attacked Port Darwin Australia, on February 19. Later in the month the carrier fleet supported the invasion of Java. Then, in an attempt to recreate the success of Pearl Harbor, elements of the fleet headed for Ceylon, striking at Colombo on April 5 and Trincomalee on April 9. While the attacks were a success from the Japanese point of view, the element of surprise was missing. For the first time the carrier-based Zero-Sens had an almost matched fight on their hands when intercepting British Hurricanes and Fulmars held the success of the attackers to a minimum. By the time the carriers got back to Japanese Home

One of the land based Model 21's of the 3rd Group flown by a squadron commander in the Dutch Indies, April 1942. Sekai no Kokuki.

Queen of the Pacific Skies. Reisen of the 3rd Group, spring 1942. Sekai no Kokuki.

Waters in the third week of April, the pilots were the heroes of the Empire. They looked the part, for they were rugged, matured in combat, and deeply tanned from their many months in Southern waters. During the entire cruise the carrier forces never came under strong attack, and no ship was lost.

But the tide of war was imperceptively beginning to turn. The Allied forces, utterly defeated in the opening months of war, were firming up. When the Fleet carriers Shokaku and Zuikaku, plus the light carrier Shoho, of the 5th Carrier Division went to sea again the object was the invasion of Port Moresby, an Allied base on the South-eastern coast of New Guinea. Air bases there would give Japan control over New Guinea, Northern Australia and the Solomons. For the first time opposing carrier forces met in the Battle of the Coral Sea. On the morning of May 7 American carrier planes from the Yorktown and Lexington hit and sank the Shoho, with the carrier's twelve Zero-Sens going to the bottom of the sea or landing on the other carriers. The next day, the Shokaku was badly damaged and put out of action. The American carrier Lexington was also sunk, giving the Japanese a claim of victory. While the battle actually appeared to be a draw, the Port Moresby invasion attempt was stopped and the Japanese retreated for the first time in the Pacific War. The battle was a costly one, for the JNAF suffered heavy losses in pilots and aircraft. Expecting an easy victory and fighting enemy carrier pilots in close quarters for the first time, the Japanese pilots were careless. During the evening of May 7 more than one A6M2 pilot attempted to land on the American carrier Yorktown, mistaking it for the Shokaku or Zuikaku in the haze when the two

Pilots and Reisens of the 3rd Group, early 1942. Koku Asahi.

Field maintenance and repair, 3rd Group. Courtesy Richard L. Seely.

The Reisen was land-based early in its career as shown here in summer 1942. As more and more carriers were lost during the war the Reisen increasingly became primarily a land-based fighter. Asahigraph.

carrier fleets were only about 30 miles apart. The fast-thinking American signalmen tried to flag them down, but recognizing their error the Japanese pilots roared away to safety at mast height. The elusive intact Zero-Sen for American study once again got away.

By far the greatest Japanese loss was the damaged Shokaku, destined to long months under repair, for now this Fleet Carrier could not be assigned to the "Midway Operation", the long-planned decisive fleet engagement of the Pacific War, scheduled for less than a month later. Admiral Yamamoto, himself a pilot, planned to invade Midway in June 1942, and bring the American fleet out to battle. The Imperial Navy, confident of victory in whatever it undertook, couldn't wait for the Shokaku. The invasion plans proceeded, and the fleet left Japan as the largest attacking force to ever sail the high seas.

The "Midway Operation" consisted of two thrusts, with a feint in the far north at the Aleutians and the American base at Dutch Harbor. This attack was led by the Fleet Carrier Ryujo, newly

Pilots of the 3rd Group rest between flights during the invasion of the Dutch Indies. Courtesy Seiso Tachibana.

equipped with A6M2 Model 21 fighters to replace the 96 Kansen fighters in use until May, and supported by the Light Carrier Junyo, newly converted from a tourist liner and equipped with 21 Zero-Sens. Striking by surprise from 400 miles away on June 3, and again on June 4 (American time), the Japanese suffered under the extreme weather and were only able to place a total of twenty A6M2 fighters and 36 bombers over the target. Lieutenant Yoshio Shiga, commander of the fighters, regretfully reported the loss of a Zero-Sen in the First Wave attack on June 3 flown by Petty Officer Tadayoshi Koga from the Ryujo. Koga's A6M2 had been hit by a stray bullet, leading to loss of oil. Dropping behind, he followed a pre-arranged plan to land on

The victory record of the 3rd Group in its march across the Indies is suggested by the eleven "kill" marks on aircraft X-183. Courtesy Richard L. Seely.

the small island of Akutan to be picked up later by submarine. On the second day two of Junyo's fighters were lost in combat, as well as two bombers, while the Japanese pilots reported the downing of five or six American fighters. Japanese rescue subs, scouring the area, found no trace of the missing pilots and gave up the search. The carrier fleet retired without loss.

Meanwhile, far to the south, the Midway assault began. At dawn on June 4, Lieutenant Masaharu Suganami of the Soryu, a Zero-Sen flying veteran of Pearl Harbor, led the first fighter group of nine fighters each from the Soryu, Akagi, Hiryu and Kaga against Midway to support the D3A2 and B5N2 bombers. The Japanese fighters contained the American defenders and not one of the Japanese bombers was attacked. The light carriers Hosho and Zuiho, far to the rear, were used to provide anti-sub and CAP cover for the Japanese surface fleet. As the day progressed the Japanese were unable to locate the American carrier fleet, although they were under carrier aircraft attack. In a welter of confusion they armed, re-armed and again re-armed their aircraft for alternating attacks against the American fleet, Midway and the fleet again. At the height of the third re-arming the Japanese carriers were caught by American dive bombers, and the course of the Pacific War was changed in five minutes. The defending CAP Zero-Sens had just thwarted a repeated series of low-level torpedo and shallow dive-bombing attempts by the Americans, encouraged by the shouted cheers of their fellow pilots and maintenance crews watching from the carrier decks, when Douglas Dauntless bombers dropped in strings from an altitude beyond interception, and had their way with the Japanese carriers below them. The Soryu, Kaga and Akagi were mortally wounded, and later in the afternoon the Hiryu was hit again. By the morning of June 5 all four Fleet Carriers had sunk or were scuttled to avoid capture. The sole American Carrier loss was the Yorktown, and for the first time the carrier forces in the Pacific were weighted in favor of the Americans. A desperate plan to use the aircraft of the Hosho for further attacks was considered, but was dropped in favor of a Japanese retreat on June 5.

Model 11's at Saigon in Indo-China, July 1941. The wartime Japanese censor has scratched the unit identification of the 14th Group out of the negative. Courtesy Richard L. Seely.

Beginning of the End

The loss in equipment at Midway was staggering. From April 1942 through March 1943, which included the Midway losses, the JNAF expended 1,590 fighter planes while only 1,747 were delivered to the Imperial Navy. This barely met the losses at a time when the Allied strength was increasing. Not only were the carrier complements lost, but additional units as well. A "Midway Group" had even been formed for the occupation of the island, with all of the aircraft stored below deck on the Fleet Carriers sunk in the battle. Fortunately, many of the Midway pilots were saved as their aircraft were in the air. Most of them were rescued by destroyers which picked them up from the water.

A Reisen at Rabaul early in 1943. This is a still taken from a wartime Japanese propaganda movie. Courtesy Noboru Jyoko.

The greatest loss was on the Hiryu with 60 pilots killed in the battle. The survivors were taken back to Japan and reassigned to the Shokaku, Zuikaku and Ryujo to replace losses. Others went to land bases in the Solomons where they flew their now-aging Zero-Sen and its later Model 32 and Model 22 variants. Most of them were lost there.

The last major carrier use of the A6M2 was in the battle of Santa Cruz on October 26, 1942. By now the Americans had landed at Guadalcanal and the Japanese threw the carriers Shokaku, Zuikaku, Zuiho and Junyo into a battle to sever the American supply lifeline to Guadalcanal in the Eastern Solomons. Under constant attack by bombers and fighters flying extended-range missions from Rabaul, and then under Japanese carrier aircraft attack, the American position on Henderson Field on Guadalcanal held out against greatly superior forces. But a new sense of American victory was being felt, for now the Japanese loss rate of A6M2 Model 21 fighters was far exceeding the American losses. With the carriers Shokaku and Zuiho damaged beyond further use in the battle in carrier-vs.-carrier aircraft duels, the Japanese retreated. Never again would the "Zero Fighter", by now now tagged with the Allied Code Name "Zeke" (although the name "Zero" retained its popularity for the remainder of the war), be regarded as invincible, for now the Allied pilots were armed with information. A few weeks after the carrier-aircraft attacks on Dutch Harbor in the Aleutians the previous June, an American patrol plane spotted an unfamiliar shape in a bog on Akutan Island. A ground party went in, discovered that the young Japanese naval Petty Of-

Victory Power! Model 21 Reisen fighters swept the skies clean of Allied fighters in the first six months of the Pacific War. Asahigraph.

Turnabout! Wreckage of an A6M2 Model 21 on Midway Island, June 4, 1942, the turning point in the Pacific War. This is taken from an American propaganda film about the war shot by acclaimed Hollywood director John Ford. Courtesy Richard L. Seely.

Hit in the air by ground fire over Dutch Harbor in the Aleutians on June 4, 1942, with one bullet draining the oil return line, aircraft DI-108 from the carrier Ryujo crash landed on American territory. Official Navy Department.

ficer who flew it had broken his neck and died when his "Zero Fighter" flipped over on hitting the soft surface, and brought the aircraft out. It proved to be a newly-produced Zero-Sen built at Nagoya in February. In July the aircraft was under repair at the United States Naval Air Station at San Diego, California and by September it was flying in USN colors. Petty Officer Tadayoshi Koga's Model 21 from the Ryujo gave the American Navy the prize it sought so long. The first performance report was issued to American pilots on September 4, and by October 31 a full report on the "Zeke's" performance in combat was widely distributed. The many "Zero Fighter" myths were put to rest, and American pilots learned how to use their slower, less maneuverable aircraft to best advantage, for in high-speed rolls and pushovers the stronger American aircraft had it all over the lighter "Zeke."

After Santa Cruz the A6M2 Model 21 did not disappear from service, although it now became a supplemental aircraft rather than the prime combat model. An attempt was made to improve the performance of the A6M2 with a turbosupercharger, but the idea was dropped after two prototypes were tested. Newer Model 32, Model 22 and later the Model 52 variants took over the Zero-Sen production lines. Most of the later-formed Model 21 units, such as the Konoike, Tokushima, Tsuiki and Tsukuba Groups in Japan, used the Model 21 on training duties. Units stretched along the Chinese coast to Syonan, the Japanese name for Singapore, using the Model 21 for anti-submarine patrol duties as part of the 1st Escort Group, as well as training. Some of these units, including the 309th and 381st Groups at Syonan, and the 901st in China, still had Model 21's on hand at the end of the war, although many had been shipped to Japan for Special Attack purposes.

Some of the Model 21's even saw first-line combat years after passing their prime. The 601st Group received Model 21's in February 1944, and assigned them to the carriers Hokaku, Shokaku and Zuikaku in April 1944 to be used in the defense of the Marianas. The 652nd and 653rd Groups in the Marianas had the A6M2 in first-line service in June

Flown by Flight Petty Officer Tadayoshi Koga of the Ryujo, the A6M2 came in for a landing on what Koga believed to be an emergency field on Akutan Island. Official Navy Department.

1944 as fighter-bombers, with the 652nd losing six and the 653rd losing 42 out of its original 46 in the "Marianas Turkey Shoot" between June 18 and 20. When the 341st Group went to its base at Clark Field in the Philippines in the summer of 1944 it took Model 21s along for training, with examples later captured there by American invasion forces. When the 11th Group was finally disbanded at Syonan in December 1944, its pilots joined the 381st Group stationed there, while its A6M2 equipment was sent back to Japan for Kamikaze operations, the final combat use of the best known Japanese aircraft of all time.

Fighter on Floats

The possibility of war in the Pacific, based on the pressures being exerted by the Western Democracies and Japan's need for Dutch Indies oil and tin, was seriously faced by the Imperial Navy at the time the Zero-Sen made its first appearance in the A6M2 Model 11 form in 1940. The need to hold positional bases in Southern waters after the carriers had struck, and before land-based fighters could be moved in due to base construction requirements, led to the assignment of a 15-Shi specification for a floatplane fighter. Kawanishi got the developmental order while Nakajima got an interim order late in 1940 to quickly produce a stop-gap float fighter to have on hand in little over a year. To save engineering time the A6M2 Model 11 minus its landing gear was to be the design basis, and in February 1941 work began on Nakajima Project AS-1 as the A6M2-N. Nakajima engineers Tajima and Niitake used every short-cut at their command, and by December 1941 the first of four prototypes was on hand at the Yokosuka Naval Air Test center. Wind tunnel and water tank tests led to the use of the mainfloat design of the existing biplane E8N1 Type 95 Reconnaissance Seaplane "Dave", mounted on a single pylon, with fuel tankage in the float, and modified vertical tail surfaces to provide the necessary additional directional stability. On December 8 (Japanese time), only a matter of hours after the attack at Pearl Harbor, the prototype A6M2-

With wheels extended, Koga hit a bog, flipped over, and died with a broken neck. The intact fighter was found a few weeks later by an American search party. Official Navy Department.

N made its first flight. By April the fighter was in production, with experimental Model 11 prototypes scheduled for combat evaluation within weeks in the Pacific. In July the A6M2-N was officially accepted for JNAF production as the Type 2 Floatplane Fighter, Model 11. It became generally known as the 2 Suisen.

Its test of strength was soon in coming. In much the same manner as the 12-Shi A6M2 was whisked to China, the preproduction A6M2-N was sent to the Solomons. On May 3, 1942, as a prelude to what was to be the unsuccessful Port Moresby invasion, Florida Island and the harbor of Tulagi were invaded. This strategic inlet further extended Rabaul's defense perimeter and gave the JNAF a base in the Solomons that provided air cover over North-eastern New Guinea as well as the Bismark Islands behind it and the far reaches of the Solomons before it. The Yokohama Air Group, equipped with twelve of the service-test A6M2-N float fighters, was immediately moved in. By the time American carrier aircraft were counterattacking on May 4, they were being intercepted by the 2 Suisen. Surprised by the American presence, the Yokohama Air Group lost 3 or 4 of its new fighters, which were quickly replaced from Japan.

As a fighter the 2 Suisen was formidable, but as a floatplane it was a shock. Armed with two 20mm cannon and two 7.7 machine guns, the A6M2-N had a speed of 270 m.p.h. It literally outperformed its American carrier-based opposition and intercepted land-based B-17E Flying Fortress bombers as high as 20,000 feet. Because it was there and had a home base in the area, the 2 Suisen owned the skies over the Solomons. Code named "Rufe" by the Allies, the fighter soon showed up throughout the Southern Islands; in the Shortlands, Rekata Bay, Poporang in the Southern Bougainvilles and around the approaches to Rabaul. As production got moving in July 1942, with an improved model coming off the Nakajima lines beginning in December and continuing through the end of production in September 1943, the "Rufe" began to show up wherever the JNAF had water close at hand, in areas where improved airfields

Flight Petty Officer Koga's short-lived Reisen in the shops at the Naval Air Station, San Diego, in original paint prior to re-assembly, July 1942. Red "108" markings are still visible on the fin. U. S. Navy.

Analysis and flight tests quickly revealed that the phenomenal performance of the "Zero Fighter" came as a result of its unusually low power and wing loadings, with elimination of protected fuel tanks as one of the shortcuts to weight reduction. Official Navy Department.

were not available.

The most dramatic use of the "Rufe" was in the Aleutians. After Midway, Admiral Yamamoto felt it unwise to attempt to invade the Aleutians, but Naval Headquarters and his fellow officers overruled his objections. Their goal was to occupy American land and prevent any assaults or invasion attempts against northern Japan across the island-hopping land bridge stretching from Alaska to the Kuriles. Sadly underrating their enemy, the Japanese assumed that the bitter weather would restrict American counter-measures and that the 2 Suisen, in the absence of airfields, would command the skies and be able to defend the Japanese bases at Kiska and Attu. The float fighters, accompanied by EI3A2, E8N1 and F1M1 floatplanes, were ferried in during June and June 1942 by the seaplane tenders Chitose, Chiyoda, Kimikawa-maru and Kamikawa-maru.

At Kiska, the Kimikawa-maru and the Kamikawa-maru unloaded their first "Rufes" for the 5th Group in June and July. Commanded by Captain Takahashi, by July 14 the 5th Group had a dozen of the float fighters set up and in operation, plus all the support equipment and supplies to maintain the unit for an extended period. They operated out of Kiska Harbor.

They arrived none too soon. Within a week after their arrival the Japanese at Kiska were under American air attack, which only intensified as the months passed and the Americans built airstrips closer and closer to the Japanese occupied islands. Briefly capturing Attu Island, leaving it, and returning again to prevent its use as an air base, the JNAF moved the Toko Group into Attu in October supported by "Rufe" fighters. B-17E Flying Fortress, B-24 Liberator, Catalina and finally Lockheed P-38 Lightning fighter attacks against the lonely Japanese garrisons, with the P-38 seeing its first combat use in the Pacific, kept the Japanese units under constant pressure. In the early days of the Aleutians fighting the "Rufe" pilots held their own. Although there were no 2 Suisen "aces", a creditable

This prize of war would cost the Imperial Japanese Navy dearly, for within eight weeks the weaknesses of the Reisen would be known to the enemy, with the data widely distributed to Allied pilots. Official Navy Department.

The clean lines of the aircraft, and the simple carrier landing gear, impressed the American technicians who studied the aircraft. They reported it was "...built like a fine watch." Official Navy Department.

number of American bombers were downed by the fast floatplanes. On at least one occasion a "Rufe" downed a P-38, in spite of the fact that the American fighter definitely held the advantage. Over Kiska, the 5th Group maintained CAP cover with two "Rufes" throughout the day, with two more going up as soon as the patrol on duty started down. By September 1942 the top ranking "Rufe" pilot at Kiska had shot down two B-17's. On September 14 the tide definitely turned. Mounting a heavy raid of twelve B-24's supported by twenty-eight P-38 and P-39 fighters, the American Army Air Forces destroyed four "Rufes" without combat loss although two of the P-38's collided and crashed.

Attacks almost daily, and continued strafing of the Japanese fighters, broke the back of the resistance. By March 1943 the frequently reinforced 5th, later the 452nd, and Toko Group were inoperable. At one point seven "Rufes" were sunk or beached at Kiska, beyond repair, while the strafed wreckage of other "Rufes" littered Holtz Bay at Attu. When American forces landed at Attu in May 1943 there was no fighter opposition. By August the Americans landed at Kiska, only to discover that the entire Japanese force had moved out under cover of fog the month before and escaped unscathed. A wrecked "Rufe" was pulled out of the sea at Attu in June, shipped to the Alameda Naval Air Station in California for study, and then soon forgotten. Pilots in the superior Allied aircraft no longer worried about the makeshift fighter.

In the South Pacific, the 2 Suisen suffered equally hard with the men of the Yokohama Air Group, first unit equipped with the fighter, becoming national martyrs. Continually on the offensive, and almost as consistently winning, the Imperial Navy was totally unprepared for any Allied counterattack. On August 7, 1942 it came, and the target was the outer reaches of the Solomons. Just before dawn the garrison at Tulagi reported that Florida and Guadalcanal islands were under heavy bombardment. When communications stopped 8th

Test pilot Commander C. T. Booth of Anacostia, D. C., prepares to take up the captured "Zeke" at San Diego for its press introduction, October 15, 1942. Official Navy Department.

The feared Japanese fighter was flown across a touchy United States from San Diego, California, to Anacostia, D. C. late in 1942, yet not a single spotter identified it as a Japanese aircraft. Official Navy Department.

Fleet Headquarters at Rabaul could only assume that Tulagi and the Yokohama Group had been completely overrun. American landings had been made, all eight of the Yokohama's "Rufes" were destroyed, and the brutal battle for control of Guadalcanal and the Solomons had begun.

With the outer fringes of Japan's wartime empire cauterized the "Rufe" was no longer the advance representative of the JNAF in the air. Its role became defensive and largely passive. In the combat zones, with the transport carrier Kaiyo supplying the 958th Group at Rabaul, the A6M2-N still found use as an interceptor until the pull-out early in 1944. At Paramushiro in the Kuriles the remnants of the 452nd Group flew interception missions from their base at Shimushu in 1942 and 1943, flying a dozen "Rufes." Farther back behind the Pacific front, "Rufes" of the 40th Group, later becoming the 936th, provided convoy escort, antisubmarine and reconnaissance patrol from its bases at Syonan and Brunei in North Borneo until the end of the war. The 801st, formerly the Yokohama Group, and the Otsu Group in Japan were also used for patrol, while the "Rufes" of the Otsu Group even doubled as B-29 interceptors late in 1944 from their base on Lake Biwa near Kyoto. Some of the late model A6M2-N fighters, 73 of which were completed in a rush in September 1943 to terminate production, had full night flying gear for patrol duties. Others became trainers for the powerful Kawanishi N1K1 Kyofu floatplane fighter "Rex", entering service early in 1945. A few even survived the war, with at least one of the 936th Group "Rufes" ultimately serving under French colors in Indo-China until the early 1950s.

Trainer for Two

The expanded training requirements of the Pacific War led to the only non-combatant model of

The captured "Zeke" was only four months old when found. Data on the aircraft noted that it was produced by Mitsubishi at Nagoya in February 1942. Official Navy Department.

The official October 31, 1942 test report from Anacostia stated the A6M2 Model 21 was "Superior to the F4F (Wildcat) in speed and climb," but "...far inferior to the F4U-1 (Corsair) in level and diving speeds." Official Navy Department.

the A6M2 Zero-Sen series. Two airframes modified to carry an instructor to the rear and student in front were produced at the 21st Naval Air Arsenal at Omura early in 1942 in much the same manner as the A5M4-K had been developed from the A5M4 fighter. Assigned a 1942 17-Shi project number, the high-speed trainer was accepted for production as the A6M2-K later in the year, strangely retaining the Type 0 production designation as the Type 0 Trainer-Fighter Model 10. Officially named the Reirensen, it became known as the Zero-Ren. The cannon and wheel covers of the combat model were removed to save weight, although the machine guns were retained for training. The 21st Arsenal put the new trainer into production late in 1942 and ultimately produced 236 more between February 1943 and October 1944. An improved model entered production at Hitachi early in 1944 with 272 produced there between May 1944 and the end of July, 1945. The Imperial Navy placed orders with Hitachi for 665 of the trainers in this period, but bombings and the inability to set up the lines fast enough caused the firm to lose over half of this potential business.

Physically, the A6M2-K looked much like its Zero-Sen parent, although a long canopy to protect the instructor (while leaving the student out in the open air) and horizontal fins on the fuselage to control an annoying tail flutter altered its appearance somewhat. The availability of the new conversion trainer enabled the JNAF to undertake an experiment in training that would hopefully speed up the process. A6M2-K trainers were assigned to combat units and students were then assigned directly to these units after completion of primary and intermediate training. The goal was to conduct all conversion training in the line units, thereby shaving three to six months from a 1-1/2 year training schedule. With pilots of natural ability the idea worked, but in the main the procedure took longer, wasted valuable fuel, and led to many unfortunate accidents. By late 1944 an acute shortage of fuel curtailed this advanced training and the on-the-job training program in combat units was re-evaluated. Fuel was allocated to the training establishments, and soon the pilots had been cut to 15 flying hours

Results of the tests were felt instantly. Preliminary test results in September and comprehensive reports in November told Allied pilots how to fight and beat the Zero-Sen. Official Navy Department.

Retouched photo of the captured "Zeke" for aircraft recognition purposes has incorrect placing of the Japanese Hinomaru (Sun Circle) markings. Many of these misleading photos were published during the Pacific War years in American, British, Commonwealth and foreign publications. Official Navy Department.

per month. Most units retained Zero-Ren trainers as pilot refreshers, while others used them for Special Attack training for the mass suicide missions anticipated in the event of an invasion of Japan. The A6M2-K held the distinction of being the last development of the famous A6M2 series to remain in production with the last example completed less than three weeks before the end of the war. Few World War II aircraft maintained such a record.

Photos of the captured "Zeke" were retouched to add the Japanese insignia for IFF recognition training and wartime manuals. Official Navy Department.

The "Tiger Zeke" captured in China provided a second test machine. Tested for over two years, it was frequently repainted depending on the tests being conducted. As EB-2 at Wright Field it carried the short-lived red-outlined American markings of 1943. USAAF Official.

Classic side view of the A6M2 Type 0 Carrier Fighter, Model 21. Held by the U. S. Army Air Force, it was subjected to new tests against U.S.A.A.F. aircraft. USAAF Official.

One of the unique features of the Model 21 was the simplified manual wingtip folding for carrier storage. It was retained in the later, more powerful A6M3 Model 22. USAAF Official.

In the air under U.S.A.A.F. test at Wright Field, Ohio, summer 1943. USAAF Official.

Captured by the Flying Tigers in China, and camouflaged in accordance with Chinese Air Force custom, the "Tiger-Zeke" was identified as P-5016, or "Captured Pursuit No. 16." USAAF Official.

Deadly view of the Zero-Sen. A head-on shot of EB-2 at Wright Field. USAAF Official.

Because of their captured A6M2, A.V.G. pilots could test fly their opposition before they met it in combat. USAAF Official.

P-5016 was flown as a test hack by the 23rd Pursuit Group, 14th Air Force, pilots for their own enemy combat evaluation. Shown here at Kunming, China along with an A.V.G. Republic P-43 Lancer and a wing of Curtiss P-40K Tomahawk fighters. USAAF Official.

When the A.V.G. became the 23rd Fighter Group of the 14th Air Force in July 1942 the "Tiger-Zeke" received U.S.A.A.F. insignia, although the Chinese colors and P-5016 markings were retained. USAAF Official.

The "Tiger-Zeke" captured Japanese fighter in Chinese insignia shows its paces in a test flight with a Republic P-43 Lancer of the A.V.G. Flying Tigers in South China, summer 1942. USAAF Official.

As the Imperial Japanese navy settled into its conquests, new land-based fighter units were formed. These are Model 21's of the 6th Group at Rabaul, New Britain, summer, later to be reassigned for a short stay at Buin, New Guinea. Courtesy Richard L. Seely.

Japan's top "Aces" meet the press when they served together in the Lae Wing of the Tainan Group, Lae, New Guinea, late 1942. Left to right (back row) are Saburo Sakai, leading World War 2 Japanese "Ace," Seiji Ishikaswa, reporter Hajima Yoshida of Yomiuri Press, and Toshio Ota, who later died with over 40 "kills" to his credit; (front row) Sadao Vehara, an unidentified JNAF pilot, and pilots Nemoto and Yoshimura. Courtesy Richard L. Seely.

Remnant of a recent past. An A6M2 wreck of the Tainan Group is found at Lae, New Guinea, in September 1943. The tide of empire had turned. Courtesy Richard L. Seely.

Jungle grass grows fast and high over the remains of a Model 21 at Gasmata, New Britain. Australian War Memorial.

The Southwest Pacific battle area was a graveyard for the cream of the Imperial Navy's pilots. This is a splashed Model 21 in the Solomons. Courtesy Warren E. Woolman.

Wreckage of an A6M2 on Bougainville Island, November 1942. Courtesy Richard L. Seely.

Poised for greatness. A wrecked "Zeke" soon became a mark of a squadron's success in the air, and a necessary unit "mascot." Courtesy Peter Selinger.

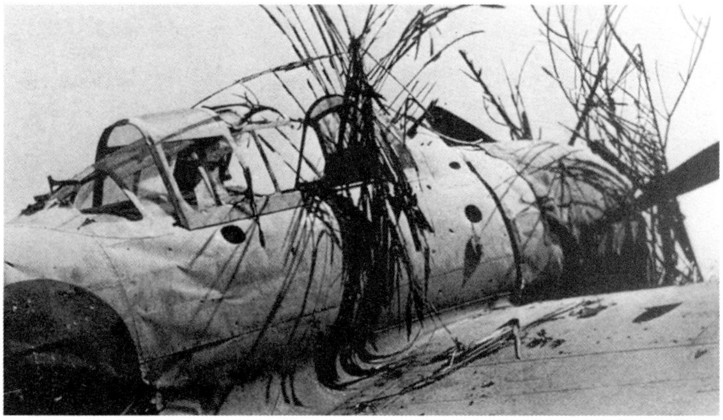

Partially intact "Zeke" fighters were found strung across the Southwest Pacific as the American "Island Hopping" campaign slowly began to reverse the Japanese gains. Courtesy Richard L. Seely.

Once the Japanese tide was checked, and then countered in the SWPA, souvenir photos of Americans standing in front of the Japanese wreckage sent to the folks back home became commonplace. Here is a Reisen wing used as a roadsign. Courtesy J. Earl Capron.

As the Guadalcanal campaign continued, and Rabaul came under attack, the A6M2 found the demands for its presence beyond its capabilities. Sekai no Kokuki.

An A6M2 floats in for a landing under power. Long wing span gave the aircraft a remarkable flight control. Courtesy M. Toda.

Japanese naval pilots, after less than a year of the luxury of air control, soon came to regard their A6M2 aircraft as inferior and dangerous when facing the newer Allied fighters entering the Pacific area. Courtesy Noboru Jyoko.

The man under the gun by the end of 1942 was the Japanese Naval Reisen pilot as Allied air power grew and the A6M series hung on to remain as the most numerically significant defender of Japanese occupied skies over its newly acquired empire. Courtesy Richard L. Seely.

Land camouflage replaced sea colors by late 1942 as Japan lost the initiative. Reisens of the 3rd Group at Timor, in the Indies "North of Australia", November 1942. Imperial Navy.

Wreckage of a Model 21 in sea colors of the 252nd Group in the Marshall Islands, February 1944. Courtesy Jack D. Canary.

Aircraft delivery of the Model 21, spring 1943, believed to be on the flight deck of the carrier Junyo. Sekai no Kokuki.

Transitional trainer A6M2 of the Konoike Group, summer 1944. Courtesy M. Toda.

In later war years many of the Model 21 fighters were assigned to trainer duties. This Reisen is the "heavy mount" at a school largely equipped with Mitsubishi A5M4 96 Kansen trainers, January 1943. Hiko Shonen.

Operated from carriers, the Model 21 was pressed into service as a fighter-bomber, shown here carrying a pair of 50 kg. frag bombs. Hiko Nippon.

Aircraft No. 101 of the Operational Training Squadron taxies past the hangars at Kasumigaura. Rarely visible Mitsubishi K3M Type 90 Operations Trainer "Pine" can be seen in the far right background in front of a hanger. Courtesy M. Toda.

Reisen advanced trainer operated by the Imperial Navy's oldest flight school at Kasumigaura, Honshu, circa 1943. Courtesy M. Toda.

Model 21's survived flight training to be modified as Tokkotai "Body Crashing" suicide planes at Kasumigaura in the spring of 1945. Courtesy M. Toda.

A flight of Model 21 Zero-Sen fighters in the advanced trainer role at the Oita Group, early 1944. Courtesy M. Toda.

Training "Zeke" at Tsukuba Group, an operational training unit in the Eastern Defense Sector of Japan, early 1944. Courtesy M. Toda.

Beauty of line an an A6M2 at Kasumigaura used for advanced training, 1943. Courtesy M. Toda.

Head of a de-fanged fighter. Aircraft No. 27 of Oita Group Operational Training Unit in the Japanese home islands, early 1944. Courtesy Hideya Ando.

The Oita Group was located at Oita on the Inland Sea, Kyushu Island, Japan. The Model 21 fighter doubled for training and bomber interception. Courtesy M. Toda.

As the war years ground to their conclusion and the inevitability of Japan's defeat, the A6M2 remained on duty as an aging but ever present threat to attacking Allied aircraft. Courtesy M. Toda.

Wreckage of a Model 21 transitional trainer-fighter "Zeke" of the 401st Fighter Squadron, 341st Group, lays in front of a Japanese Army Air Force Ki.61 Type 3 Fighter Hien "Tony," Clark Field, at the conclusion of the Philippines campaign. Courtesy Al Schmidt.

A6M2 of the 402nd Fighter Squadron, 341st Group, with its tips folded at Clark Field line up in January 1945. JAAF Kawasaki Ki.45Kai Type 2 Two-Seat Fighter Toryu "Nick" behind it, with two more "Nicks" across the road. Courtesy Al Schmidt.

Strafing destroyed the Japanese air strength at Clark Field. Remnants, such as this 402nd Fighter Squadron Model 21 Reisen, were all that were left when the field was occupied by American forces. Courtesy Fred C. Dickey, Jr.

Last of the many, this intact Reisen Model 21 was found at the Atsugi Naval Base in Japan at the war's end. Photo was taken September 5, 1945. Official Navy Department.

Model 21 of the 401st Fighter Squadron, 341st Group located at Clark Field in the Philippines, October 23, 1944. Courtesy Peter M. Bowers.

Colorful but out of combat. A6M2 Model 21 as an operational trainer at the Konoike Air Corps Gunnery School, summer 1944. Courtesy M. Toda.

One of the last surviving Model 21 Reisens is shown in surrender green cross markings at Kiangwan Airfield, Shanghai, China, in November 1945. Kyushu-produced K3M3 Type 90 Operations Trainer "Pine" is in right of center background. Courtesy Peter M. Bowers.

Aircraft No. 106 in surrender markings at Shanghai. "Chin" marking on fin denotes assignment to coastal China for convoy escort. This example was used for advanced training and doubled as an interceptor with final use scheduled to be as a Tokkotai suicide attack aircraft. Courtesy Peter M. Bowers.

Test flown by JNAF pilots under Royal Air Force supervision at Singapore, this surviving Model 21 in British markings was in an operational and convoy escort unit at Seletar. British Official.

Both the Model 21, foreground, and the Model 52 Zero-Sen fighters were stationed at Syonan, or Singapore, for training, defense and convoy escort. British Official.

A6M2-N at Yokosuka, early 1942. This seagoing fighter interceptor was the A6M2 Model 11 airframe modified and adapted to float installation by Nakajima engineers. Mitsubishi A6M3 Model 32 Reisen "Hamp" with squared wing tips, later re-coded "Zeke 32," to the right.

Evaluation of the A6M2-N was rushed at Yokosuka in the spring of 1942. Koku Shonen.

The rudder area of the A6M2-N was modified to remove the A6M2 tail cone and provide more control area. Koku Shonen.

The Nakajima-built A6M2-N "Rufe" had the solid wingtips of the Reisen Model 11 airframe to stand up to the rigors of forward base use, shown here at Yokosuka testing. Courtesy Richard L. Seely.

Production of the 2 Suisen "Rufe" began in April 1942. Over a hundred were produced during the next nine months of the year. Sekai no Kokuki.

The 2 Suisen was the first new fighter to be met in combat in the Pacific that reached production status after Pearl Harbor. Sekai no Kokuki.

2 Suisen color schemes ranged from jungle camouflage to sea colors. This unit is operational in spring 1943. Umi to Sora.

Looking ungainly in the air, the "Rufe" still outperformed its opposition until the introduction of newer Allied fighters late in 1942. Kokutisiki.

The 2 Suisen provided positional fighter cover where airfields did not yet exist, giving the Imperial Navy a decided advantage in forward areas. The Allies had no comparable aircraft. Hiko Nippon.

Prototype A6M2-N was first test flown on the day of the Pearl Harbor raid, Monday in Japan. By July 1942 it was in combat. Umi to Sora.

The 958th Group at Rabaul flew "Rufes" until the base was evacuated in February 1944. Umi to Sora.

Over the jungles of Florida Island the "Rufes" of the Yokohama Air Corps are difficult to spot. Koku Shonen.

Hidden by the jungle, "Rufes" of the Yokohama Group adjust to their beach base in the Solomon Islands. Koku Asahi.

The first A6M2-N unit to go operational, the Yokohama Group came under the command of the 25th Air Flotilla at Rabaul. Courtesy Richard L. Seely.

The Yokohama Group was completely wiped out before dawn on August 7, 1942 by American carrier aircraft when its base got caught in the crunch of the American invasion of Guadalcanal. Imperial Navy.

Quiet days at Tulagi, June 1942, before the American invasion of Guadalcanal. Koku Asahi.

A carefully maintained 2 Suisen basking in the "Southern Islands" just prior to the American invasion of the Solomons, summer 1942. Koku Asahi.

The 5th Group received its first "Rufes" in July 1942 to equip its forward base at Attu in the Aleutians. Sekai no Kokuki.

Eight "Rufes" arrived at Kiska aboard the Kamikawa-maru on June 15, 1942 and were used for air cover. Sekai no Kokuki.

"Rufes" aboard the Kamikawa-maru early in June, 1942, being rushed to the Aleutians for air cover. Courtesy Richard L. Seely.

The same "Rufes" spotted in Holtz Bay by American reconnaissance planes in August 1942. USAAF Official.

"Rufes" from the Kamikawa-maru being set up on the beach at Holtz Bay, Attu, in August 1942. Kawanishi H6K2 Type 97 Flying-Boat "Mavis" command flying boat of the Toko Group in the far background. Imperial Navy.

During the 1943-1944 period the "Rufe" was assigned convoy escort duties with the 801st and 936th Group. Koku Asahi.

The only Japanese fighter aircraft to be based on captured American soil (or at least water), the 2 Suisen immediately ruled the skies over the western Aleutians and created a major problem for American strategists. Courtesy Richard L. Seely.

Available in an improved model in some numbers by early 1943, "Rufe" equipped other advance air defense units. Sekai no Kokuki.

Outclassed by allied land-based fighters by late 1942, the A6M2-N ruled the skies in areas where no landing fields existed. Sekai no Kokuki.

Brought out for Home Island air defense duties when the B-29 raids began, late model "Rufes" of the Otsu Group were stationed on Lake Biwa near Kyoto in late 1944. Koku Asahi.

Former 936th Group "Rufe" at Seletar, Singapore, test flown by Allied Air Intelligence Unit (ATAIU) of the RAF. Aircraft was later turned over to the French in Indo-China. British Official.

A mixed bag of single-seat A6M2 and two-seat A6M2-K trainers of the Genzan Group operational training school at Genzan, Chosen (Wonsan, North Korea) in the fall of 1944. Courtesy M. Toda.

Utilizing the wings and tail of the A6M2 Model 11, the A6M2-K had a modified two-seat fuselage. Courtesy Hideya Ando.

Tainan Group Zero-Rensen trainers in October 1944 after the unit's return to Formosa from Truk. Sekai no Kokuki.

The last act! Zero-Rensen trainers being wheeled out of their hangar, Fall 1945, to be destroyed in accordance with surrender terms. Courtesy Richard L. Seely.

Flight of late model A6M2-K trainers of the Tsukuba Group on a training flight in 1944. Courtesy M. Toda.

Bright orange target-tow A6M2-K of the Konoike Group in the summer of 1944. Tow cans are under wings. Courtesy M. Toda.

Camouflaged Hitachi-built A6M2-K trainers, center rear, used for operation training for conversion to the new N1K1-J Shiden fighters, left, of the Genzan Group, Chosen, early 1945. Courtesy Richard L. Seely.

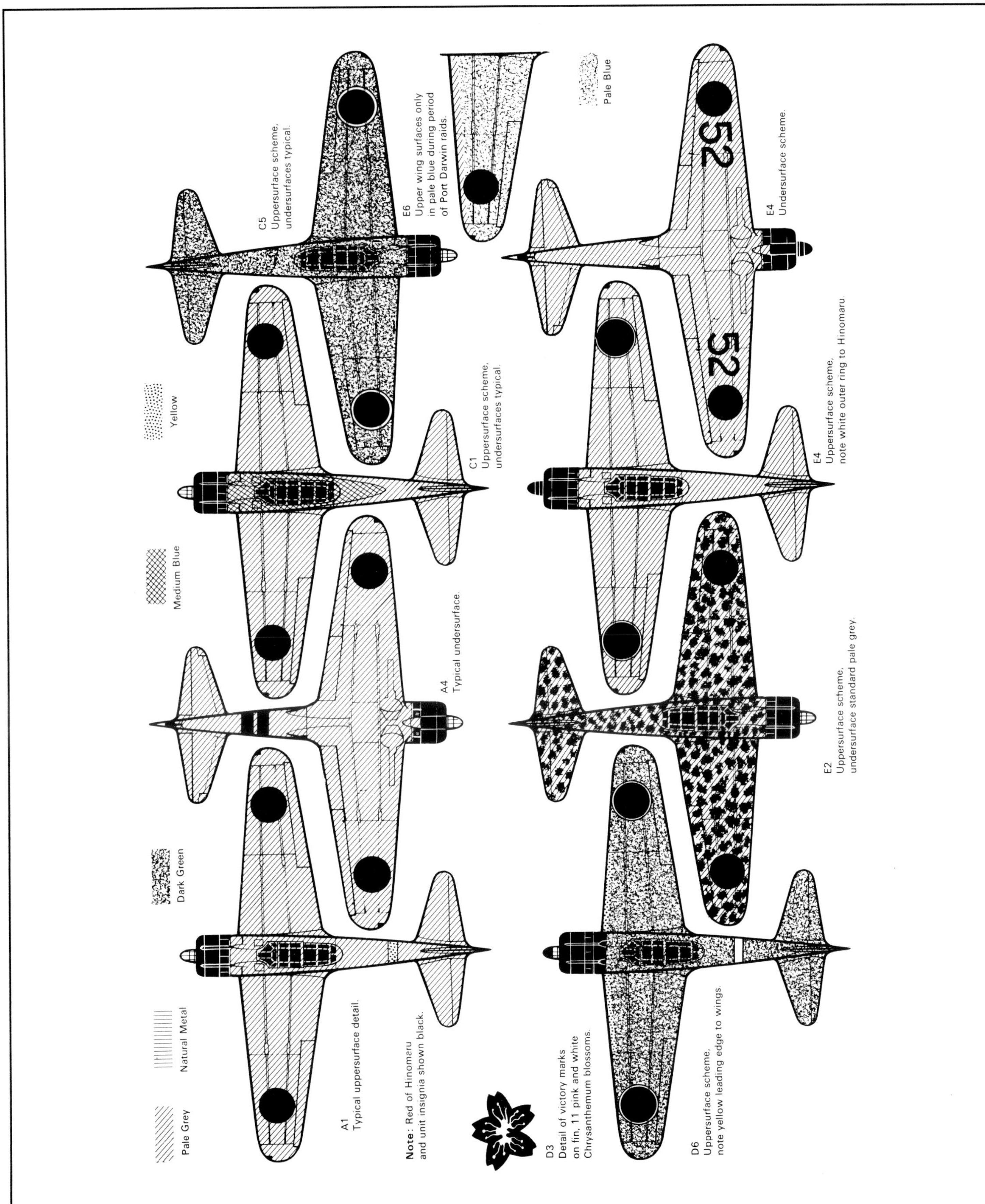

Pale Grey
Natural Metal
Dark Green
Medium Blue
Yellow
Pale Blue
A1
Typical uppersurface detail.
Note: Red of Hinomaru and unit insignia shown black.
A4
Typical undersurface.
C1
Uppersurface scheme, undersurfaces typical.
C5
Uppersurface scheme, undersurfaces typical.
E6
Upper wing surfaces only in pale blue during period of Port Darwin raids.
D3
Detail of victory marks on fin, 11 pink and white Chrysanthemum blossoms.
D6
Uppersurface scheme, note yellow leading edge to wings.
E2
Uppersurface scheme, undersurface standard pale grey.
E4
Uppersurface scheme, note white outer ring to Hinomaru.
E4
Undersurface scheme.
52
52

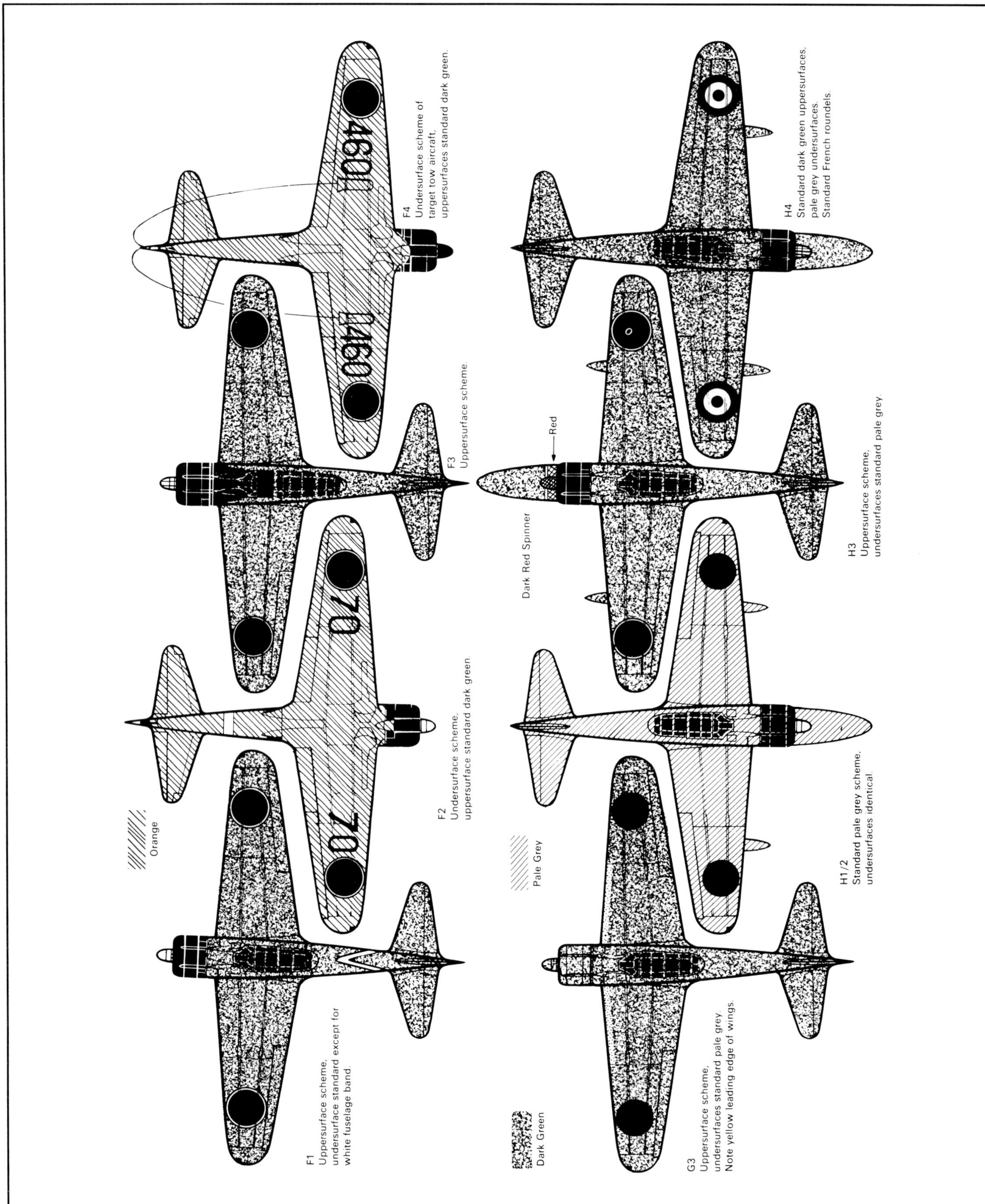
Orange
Pale Grey
Dark Green
Dark Red Spinner
Red
70
70
4601
1460
F1
Uppersurface scheme,
undersurface standard except for
white fuselage band.
F2
Undersurface scheme,
uppersurface standard dark green
F3
Uppersurface scheme.
F4
Undersurface scheme of
target tow aircraft,
uppersurfaces standard dark green.
G3
Uppersurface scheme,
undersurfaces standard pale grey.
Note yellow leading edge of wings.
H1/2
Standard pale grey scheme,
undersurfaces identical.
H3
Uppersurface scheme,
undersurfaces standard pale grey.
H4
Standard dark green uppersurfaces,
pale grey undersurfaces.
Standard French roundels.

IMPERIAL JAPANESE NAVAL AIR FORCE (UNAF)
UNITS OPERATING A6M2 Zero-Sen (Reisen)

IMPERIAL NAVY CARRIERS

Carrier	When used	Area of Operations	Former A/C	Later A/C	Comments
Akagi Dec. 8, 1941: 1st Air Fleet 1st Carrier Div. 1st Carrier	April 1941- June 1942	Pearl Harbor, Hawaii Rabaul, New Britain Indian Ocean Midway	A2N A4N A5M	None	Flagship of Nagumo Fleet, Pearl Harbor attack. Carried 18 A6M2, 18 D3A2, 27 B5N2 total 63 aircraft. Fighter commands were Lieut cmdr. Itaya, 1st wave: Lieut. Shindo, 2nd wave At Midway, Itaya again Fighter commander. Lost at Midway June 5, 1942.
Chuyo *(Nitta-maru)*	Nov 1942- Dec 1943	Home Islands Southern Seas	None	A6M3	Training carrier. Former N.Y K. liner *Nitta-maru* converted May Nov 1942 Ferried aircraft to Pacific bases, 50-60 aircraft per trip. Delivered A6M2 to Truk, Rabaul, etc. Launched deliveries at sea. Sunk by sub Dec 4, 1943.
Hiryu Dec. 8. 1941: 1st Air Fleet 2nd Carrier Div. 2nd Carrier	April 1941- June 1942	Pearl Harbor, Hawaii Wake Island Port Darwin Indian Ocean Midway	A5M	None	Commissioned in 1940. Carried 18 D3A2, 18 B5N2. Rated up to 63-73 aircraft. At Midway carrier commander Captain Tomeo Kaku. Fighters under Lieut. Shigeru Mori. Carried "Midway Expeditionary Force" A6M2 aircraft. Sunk at Midway, June 5, 1942.
Hiyo *(Izumo-maru)* July 14, 1942: 3rd Air Fleet 2nd Carrier Div. 2nd Carrier	July 1942- early 1943	North Solomons Rabaul, New Britain Truk	None	A6M3 A6M5 A6M7	Light carrier Former N.Y.K liner *Izumo-maru* converted summer 1942. Rated at 53 aircraft. Carried 21 A6M2, 18 D3A2, 9 B5N2 in Solomons. Saw much action in Solomons. Rabaul. Later in 4th and 2nd Carrier divisions.
Hosho	Feb. 1942- end of war	Home Islands Midway Home Islands	10 Kansen A1N A2N A4N A5M	A6M2- K	Light escort and training carrier. Built Dec. 27,1922. Carried 15 aircraft. First Japanese carrier. Anti-sub escort and patrol at Midway. Recovered A6M2 from lost carriers at Midway. Carrier training thereafter. Survived war to be scrapped.
Junyo *(Kashiwara-maru)* July 14, 1942: 3rd Air Fleet 2nd Carrier Div. 1st Carrier	May 1942- early 1943	Aleutians SantaCruz North Solomons	None	A6M3 A6M5 A6M7	Light carrier. Former N.Y.K. liner *Kashiwara-maru* converted summer 1942. Rated at 53 aircraft. Carried 21 A6M2, 18 D3A2, 9 B5N2 in Solomons. In Aleutians was 4th Carrier Div., 2nd Carrier. Commander Captain Geito Ishii. Saw much action.

Carrier	When used	Area of Operations	Former A/C	Later A/C	Comments
Kaga Dec. 8, 1941: 1st Air Fleet 1st Carrier Div. 2nd Carrier	April 1941- June 1942	Pearl Harbor. Hawaii Rabaul, New Britain Indian Ocean Midway	A2N A4N A5M A6M1	None	A6M1 *12-Shi* carrier acceptance trials on *Kaga* in June 1940. Saw much action. Carried 72 aircraft. At Midway had 21 A6M2, 27 D3A2, 18 B5N2. Carrier commander Captain Jisaku Okada. Fighter commander Lieut Masao Sato. Sunk at Midway June 4, 1942.
Ryujo July 14, 1942: 3rd Air Fleet 2nd Carrier Div. 3rd Carrier	June 1942- Aug. 1942	Aleutians North Solomons Eastern Solomons	A2N A4N A5M	None	Last major carrier to convert to A6M2. Flagship of Aleutians invasion and attack force. Carried 24 A6M2, 9 B5N2 Rated at 48 aircraft. First captured "Zeke" came from Ryujo. Carrier commander Captain Tadao Kato. Sunk in Eastern Solomons Aug 24. 1942.
Shoho *(Tsurugizaki)*	Feb. 1942- May 1942	Rabaul, New Britain Tulagi, Solomons Coral Sea	A5M4	None	Former sub tender converted to carrier in Jan.1942. Light carrier first equipped with A5M4 fighters, soon dropped for A6M2. Ferried aircraft to Rabaul. Carried 30 aircraft. In Battle of Coral Sea had 12 A6M2 and 12 B5N2. Sunk at Coral Sea May 8,1942.
Shokaku Dec. 8, 1941: 1st Air Fleet 5th Carrier Div. 1stCarrier	Sept. 1941- early 1943	Pearl Harbor, Hawaii Rabaul, New Britain Indian Ocean Port Moresby, New Guinea. Coral Sea Santa Cruz	None	A6M3	Saw much action. At Pearl Harbor carried 18 A6M2, 27 D3A2, 27 B5N2. Rated at 84 aircraft. Carried 75. On July 14, 1942 became 3rd Air Fleet, 1st Carrier Div. Then carried 27 A6M2, 27 D3A2, 18 B5N2. Damaged in Coral Sea so not at Midway.
Soryu Dec. 8, 1941: 1st Air Fleet 2nd Carrier Div 1st Carrier	April 1941- June 1942	Pearl Harbor, Hawaii Wake Isand Indian Ocean Midway	A4N A5M	None	Saw much action. At Pearl Harbor carried 18 A6M2, 18 D3A2, 18 B5N2. Rated at 63 aircraft At Midway Air Officer Commander Takashige Egusa. Fighters under Lieut. Masaharu Suganami. Carried "Midway Expeditionary Force" A6M2 aircraft. Sunk at Midway June 4, 1942.
Taiyo *(Kasuga-maru)* July 14, 1942: Combined Fleet 3rd Carrier Div. 2nd Carrier	Jan. 1942- Middle 1943	Home Islands Southern Seas	A5M4	A6M3	Light carrier Laid down as N.Y.K. liner *Kasuga-maru.* Converted to A6M2 in 1942. Renamed *Taiyo* August 1942. Ferried aircraft to Southern Seas. Unsuitable as Fleet Carrier. On July 14, 1942 carried 11 A6M2 and 14 D1A2. Rated at 27 aircraft Became Training Carrier.

Carrier	When used	Area of Operations	Former A/C	Later A/C	Comments
Unyo (Yawata-maru) July 14, 1942: Combined Fleet 3rd Carrier Div 1st Carrier	July 1942- middle 1943	Home Islands Rabaul, New Britain Southern Seas Solomons	None	A6M3	Light carrier. Laid down as N.Y K liner *Yawata-maru* Oct. 1939. Converted as carrier Jan.-May 1942. Renamed Unyo in August 1942 Ferried aircraft to Southern Seas. Unsuitable as Fleet Carrier. Rated at 27 aircraft. Carried 50-60 as ferry to Truk.
Zuiho July 14,1942: 3rd Air Fleet 5th Carrier Div 3rd Carrier	May 1942- early 1943	Home Islands Midway Santa Cruz Rabaul, New Britain	A5M4	A6M3 A6M5 A6M7	Light escort carrier. At Midway carried 12 A6M2 and 12 B5N2 in Kondo Force for anti-subpatrol. Normally carried 21 A6M2, 6 B5N2. Rated at 30 aircraft. Fighters under Lieut. Moriyasu Hidaka. In Southern Seas Oct. 1942 was 1st Carrier Div., 3rd Carrier.
Zuikaku Dec. 8, 1941: 1st Air Fleet 5th Carrier Div 2nd Carrier	Sept 1941- early 1943	Pearl Harbor, Hawaii Rabaul, New Britain Indian Ocean Port Moresby, New Guinea, Coral Sea Santa Cruz	None	A6M3 A6M5	Saw much action. At Pearl Harbor carried 18 A6M2, 27 D3A2, 27 B5N2. Carried 75 aircraft. On July 14, 1942 became 3rd Air Fleet, 1st Carrier Div. Then carried 27 A6M2, 27 D3A2, 18 B5N2. In Southern Pacific was 2nd Carrier in Division.

NAVAL AIR GROUPS

Naval Air Groups	When used	Area of Operations	Former A/C	Later A/C	Comments
Chitose July 14, 1942 11th Air Fleet 24th Air Flotilla	Middle 1941- Nov. 1942	Home Islands "Inner South Seas" (Kwajalein and Wake) Solomons	A5M	None	On July 14,1942 unit flew 36 A6M2 and 36 G4M1. Home base at Chitose, Ishikari, Hokkaido Island. In support of Midway ops stationed at Kwajalein in June 1942 under command of Captain Fujiro Ohashi. Later became part of 653rd Group.
Genzan July 14, 1942: 11th Air Fleet 22nd Air Flotilla	Sept. 1, 1941- Aug. 1942	Genzan, Chosen Saigon, Indo-China Malaya Rabaul, New Britain	A5M	A6M2-K N1 K1-J N1 K2-J	On July 14, 1942 unit flew 36 A6M2 and 36 G4M1. Home base at Genzan, Chosen (Wonsan, North Korea). Fighters were attached to unit. 18 combat, 6 reserve A6M2 assigned to 22nd Air Flotilla. Fighters under Capt Kameo Sonokawa.
Hyakuri Dec. 8, 1941: Yokosuka Force 11th Combined Air Flotilla	Early 1942- end of war	Home Islands	A5M	None	Operational training unit. On Dec. 8, 1941 was part of Second Line striking force, flying 108 training aircraft Also known as *Hyakurihara* and *Hyakuri-gahara*. Part of Yokosuka Naval Station Force.

Naval Air Groups	When used	Area of Operations	Former A/C	Later A/C	Comments
Kanoya July 14, 1942: SW Area Fleet 21st Air Flotilla	Fall 1941- late 1942	Home Islands Saigon, Indo China Buin, Solomons	A5M	None	Combat unit. Flew A6M2 and G4M1. On July 14, 1942 had 36 A6M2. Home base Kanoya, Kagoshima, Kyushu. Covered Malaya invasion.
Kasumigaura Dec. 8, 1941: Yokosuka Force 11th Combined Air Flotilla	Fall 1941- end of war	Kasumigaura, Honshu Home Islands	10 Kansen A1N A2N A3N A4N A5M	None	Operational training unit. Formed at *Kasumigaura* Ibaragi, Honshu in 1922. Part of Second Line striking force Dec. 8, 1941, flying 164 trainers A6M2 transition training. Aircraft later stripped for Special Attack.
Konoike	Feb 1944- Dec. 1944	Home Islands	None	A6M5	Operational training unit. Flew A6M2 in training throughout 1944. Also flew A6M5c as fighter. A6M2 aircraft later assembled for Special Attack use in event of Home Islands invasion.
"Midway" April 1942: 11 th Air Fleet	April 1942- June 5, 1942	Home Islands Midway	None	None	To be stationed at Midway as land based Air Corps Known as Midway Expeditionary Force. 36 A6M2 under Lt Cmdr. Mitsugu Kokofuda carried to Midway on carriers *Akagi* ,*Kaga, Soryu Hiryu*. All lost in Midway battle. Invasion scheduled June 6, 1942.
Oita Dec. 8, 1941: Kure Force 12th Air Flotilla	Fall 1941- March 1944	Oita, Kyushu Home Islands	A5M A5M4-K	A6M2-K	Operational training unit. Part of Second Line striking force Dec 8, 1941 flying 52 A6M2 and 24 A5M4 Fighter Trainers. Home base at *Oita* (also *Ohita)* Oita pref. Kyushu on the Inland Sea.
Ominato Dec. 8. 1941: Ominato Force	Fall 1941- early 1943	Home Islands	A5M	Unknown	Combat unit. Part of Second Line striking force on Dec 8, 1941 flying A6M4, A6M2, B5N2, E13A1. Home base at Ominato, Aomori (Mutsu Bay), Honshu. Part of Ominato Naval Station Force.
Omura Dec 8. 1941: Kure Force 12th Air Flotilla	Late 1941- end of war	Omura, Kyushu (Middle Defense Sector)	A5M	A6M2-K A6M5-K	Combat unit. Part of Second Line striking force Dec. 8, 1941 flying 36 A5M4 and A6M2. Became Operational Training unit late 1942. "Ace" Saburo Sakai instructor, March 1943. Home base was *Omuro* (also *Ohmura)* Nakasaki, Kyushu. Assigned to Middle Defense Sector.

Naval Air Groups	When used	Area of Operations	Former A/C	Later A/C	Comments
Saeki Dec. 8, 1941: Kure Force	Middle 1942- end of war	Home Islands	A5M	Unknown	Combat unit. Part of Second Line striking force on Dec. 8, 1941 with 2-seat seaplanes. Later assignment included A6M2. Part of Kure Naval Station Force. Also known as *Saheki.* Based at Saaeki. Oita, Kyushu.
Tainan Dec. 8, 1941: 11th Air Fleet 23rd Air Flotilla	Sept. 1941- Nov. 1942	Tainan, Taipei Philippines Dutch East Indies Lae & Buna, New Guinea, Rabaul, New Britain, Home Islands	A5M A6M2-K	A6M	Crack combat unit. Had 92 A6M2 on Dec 8. 1941. Attacked Philippines from Taipei (Formosa) More "Aces" than any JNAF unit. Arrived Rabaul April 1942. July 14, 1942 in 11th Air Fleet, 25th Air Flotilla. Became 251st Air Groups, Japan, Nov 1942.
Tokushima 2nd Air Fleet	Summer 1943- end of war	Tokushima, Shikoku Home Islands Okinawa	A5M	A6M3 A6M2-K	Operational training unit. Home base at Tokushima, Tokushima Prefecture, Shikoku. Loss of carriers in 3rd and 4th Carrier Div. in Oct. 1944 enlarged unit by both aircraft and pilots. Combat training in Inland Sea not completed. Flew trainers for Special Attack.
Tsuiki	Oct. 1942- Feb. 1945	Home Islands 1945	A5M A5M4- K	None	Primary and transitional pilot training school. Flew A6M2 for conversion to A6M5 and A6M7 in combat and Special Attack. Also flew K5Y1 Terminated in Feb. 1945 when unit joined 553rd Group.
Tsukuba Dec. 8, 1941: Yokosuka Force 11 th Air Flotilla		Tsukuba, Honshu Home Islands (Eastern Defense Sector)	A5M	A6M5 N1K1-J A6M2-K	Operational training unit. Part of Second Line striking force on Dec 8, 1941, flying 108 trainers. Home base at Tsukuba, Ibaragi, Honshu. Later flew fighters as part of Home Island Defense.
Yatabe Dec. 8, 1941: Yokosuka Force 11th Combined Air Flotilla	Summer 1942- Fall 1944	Yatabe, Honshu Home Islands	A5M	A6M A6M2-K	Operational training unit. School established in Dec. 1939. Part of Second Line striking force on Dec. 8, 1941 flying 108 trainers. Flew A6M2 for transitional training to later A6M3 and A6M5 models.

Naval Air Groups	When used	Area of Operations	Former A/C	Later A/C	Comments
Yokosuka Dec. 8, 1941: Yokosuka Force July 1944: 3rd Air Fleet	Summer 1941- July 1944	Yokosuka, Honshu Home Islands	A5M A5M4-K	A6M3 A6M5 A6M2-N	Combat unit. Part of second line striking force on Dec. 8, 1941. Home base at Yokosuka. Kanagawa. Honshu on Tokyo Bay. Became operational. training unit flying A5M4 and A6M2. Top "Ace" Nishizawa instructor Dec. 1942-Jan. 1943. Used A6M2 in *Kamikaze* attack, June 18, 1945.
Yokosuka Naval Air Test Centre	April 1940- late 1941	Yokosuka, Honshu	A2N A4N A5M	A6M5 A6M2-N	*Ko* marking denotes *Kukugizitsusho* (Research) aircraft used for tests, experimental and combat evaluation. Prototype aircraft tested by Yokosuka. A6M2 Model 11 test aircraft crashed in dive test April 17, 1941, killing pilot Lieut. Shimokawa.
1st Dec. 8, 1941: 11th Air Fleet 21st Air Flotilla	Sept. 1941- April 1943	Takao, Taipei "Inner South Seas" (Aur and Wotje) Solomons	None	A6M3	Crack combat unit. Had 72 A6M2 and 24 reserve on Dec. 8, 1941. In late May was assigned to Aur and Wotje to provide cover for Midway invasion. Fighters under command of Captain Samaji Inouye. Assigned to 24th Air Flotilla in July. Decimated over Guadalcanal.
3rd Dec. 8, 1941: 11th Air Fleet 23rd Air Flotilla	May 1941- Aug. 1942	French Indo China Taichu, Taipei Philippines Dutch East Indies Kendari, Celebes New Guinea	None	None	Crack combat unit. Had 92 A6M2, 72 G3M2 and 12 C5M2 on Dec. 8, 1941. Attacked Philippines from Taipei (Formosa). Small portion remained to reduce Bataan. Became part of SW Area Fleet. Under command of Captain Yoshio Kamei.
4th April 1, 1942: 25th Air Flotilla	Feb. 1942- Nov. 1942	Rabaul, New Britain "North of Australia" (Darwin) Buna, New Guinea	None	A6M3	Ferried to Rabaul by carrier *Shoho* in March 1942 Portion transferred to *Tainan* Group. 25th Air Flotilla began attacks on NE Australia from Rabaul on April 25, 1942. Flew A6M2 and G4M1. Decimated over Guadalcanal. Became 702nd Group in Nov. 1942.
6th July 14, 1942: 11th Air Fleet 26th Air Flotilla	April 1942- Nov. 1942	"Inner South Seas" (Marcus Island) Rabaul, New Britain Buin, New Guinea Truk	None	A6M3	Unit had 60 A6M2, 8 C5M2,12 L2D2 in July 1942. Assigned to provide search and cover for Midway invasion from Marcus Island. Moved to Rabaul in Fall 1942 after Guadalcanal attack. Decimated over Guadalcanal. Became 204th Group in Nov 1942.

Naval Air Groups	When used	Area of Operations	Former A/C	Later A/C	Comments
11th	Sept. 1944- Dec. 1944	Home Islands Seretar, Syonan Home Islands	None	A6M5	Unit assigned to Seretar, Syonan (Seletar, Singapore) in Sept 1944 for advance training and escort. Pilots transferred to 381st Group when aircraft returned to Japan for Kamikaze and defense use.
12th Combined	Sept. 1940- early 1942	Hankow, China French Indo-China	A4N A5M	None	First unit to receive A6M2, Model 11. Total of 15 A6M2 sent to China July 21, 1940. First "kills" Sept. 13, 1940. Under command of Lieuts. Saburo Shindo and Tamotsu Yokohama. 59 "kills" without loss by Dec. 31, 1940. Occupation of Indo-China, summer 1941.
202nd 1st Air Fleet 23rd Air Flotilla	Feb. 1942- July 1944	Occupied China Mereyon, Dutch East Indies Kendari, Celebes Koepang, Timor "North of Australia"	None	A6M3	Occupied China. Transferred to Dutch Indies in early 1942. Escort and convoy protection. Flew in raids against Merauke and Darwin, Australia spring and summer 1943. Under command of Lieut. Comdr. Suzuki Minoru. Became 301st Group.
309th	May 1944- end of war	Seretar, Syonan	None	A6M5	Operational training unit at Syonan (Singapore) as part of plan to train pilots near oil producing areas. 50 A6M2 and A6M5 aircraft and personnel assigned to unit in May 1944. Navigational training for later Special Attack use.
341st 1944: 2nd Air Fleet 26th Air Flotilla	Early 1944- end of war	Tateyama, Honshu Home Islands Clark Field, Philippines Home Islands	None	A6M5	Combat and operational training. Unit stationed at Tateyama, Chiba, Honshu, SE of Tokyo. Under command of Captain Motoharu Okamura. Fighter elements flew A6M5. Training flew A6M2. Moved to Philippines, Clark Field, Jan. 17, 1945 to become Special Attack.

SPECIFICATIONS

Mitubishi A6M Zero Ship-Based (Carrier) Fighter Reisen (Zero-Fighter) and Modifications

Note: All dimensions in original Japanese metric. Dimensions and climb in meters (m), weights in kilograms (kg), distances in kilometers (km), and speeds in kilometers – per-hour (km/hr.). Data in parenthesis are estimates or approximate.

Model and Specs	A6M1 *12-Shi* Prototypes	A6M2 *12-Shi* Prototypes	A6M2 Model 11	A6M2 Model 21	A6M2 Model 21	A6M2a Model21A
Crew	1	1	1	1	1	1
Span (M)	12.000	12.000	12.000	12.000	12.000	12.000
Length (M)	8.78	9.06	9.06	9.06	9.06	9.06
Height (M)	3.43	3.509	3.509	3.509	3.509	3.509
Wing Area $(M)^2$	22.44	22.44	22.44	22.44	22.44	22.44
Weight Empty (kg)	1,652	1,671	1,671	1,680	1,680	
Weight Loaded (kg)	2,343	2,389	2,388	2,410	2,410	
Weight Loaded Max (kg)						
Max. Speed (km/hr)	513/3600m	533/4550m	533/4550m	520/4550m	520/4550m	
Cruising Speed (km/hr)						
Climb (m/min)	5000/7' 15"	6000/7' 27"	6000/7' 27"	6000/7' 27"	6000/7' 27"	
Armament-M.G. (mm)	2 x 7.7	2x7.7	2 x 7.7	2 x 7.7	2 x 7.7	2 x 7.7
Armament-Cannon (mm)	2 x 20	2 x 20	2 x 20	2 x 20	2 x 20	2 x 20
Armament-Bombs (kg)	2 x 30, or 2 x 60	2 x 30, or 2 x 60	2 x 30, or 2 x 60	2 x 20, or 2 x 60	2 x 30, or 2 x 60	2 x 30, or 2 x 60
Power Unit-Mfr.	Mitsubishi	Nakajima	Nakajlma	Nakajima	Nakajima	Nakajima
Type	MK2 *Zuisei 13*	NK1c *Sakae 12*	NK1c *Sakae 12*	NK1c *Sakae 12*	NK1c *Sakae 12*	NK1c *Sakae 12*
H.P	780	940	940	940	940	940
Aircralt-Mfr.	Mitsubishi	Mitsubishi	Mitsubishi	Mitsubishi	Mitsubishi Nakajima	Field Modif .
First Built	March 19,1939	Dec. 1939	July 31,1940	Nov. 1940	April 17,1941	(1943)
Number Built	2	17	47*	127	(1425)**	(35)[†]

NOTES
* Reinforced wing spar beginning with aircraft No.22.
** Differed from earlier model 21 by having aileron tabs.
† Long barrel 20mm cannon.
†† Model 21 with turbosupercharger.

A6M4 Model 41	A6M2-N *15-Shi*	A6M2 Model 11	A6M2-N Model 21	A6M2-K *17-Shi*	A6M2-K Model 11	A6M2-K Model 21
1	1	1	1	2	2	2
12.000	12 000	12.000	12.000	12.000	12.000	12.000
9.06		10.10	10.131	9.150	9.150	9.150
3.509	4.30	4.30	4.305	3.509	3.509	3.509
22.44	22.44	22.44	22.44	22.44	22.44	22.44
		1,921	1,921		1,819	
		2,460	2,460		2,334	
		2,880				
			435/4000m		476	476
		3000/3' 57"	5000/6' 43"		6000/7' 56"	
2 x 7.7	2 x 7.7	2 x 7.7	2 x 7.7	2 x 7.7	2 x 7.7	2 x 7.7
2 x 20	2 x 20	2 x 20	2 x 20	—	—	—
2 x 30,or	2 x 30, or	2 x 30, or	2 x 30, or	—	—	2 x 30
2 x 60	2 x 60	2 x 60	2 x 60			
Nakajima	Nakajima	Nakajima	Nakajima	Nakajima	Nakajima	Nakajima
NK1c *Sakae 12*	NK1c *Sakae 12*	NK1c *Sakae 12*	NK1c *Sakae 12*	NK1c *Sakae 12*	NK1c *Sakae 12*	NK1c *Sakae 12*
940	940	940	940	940	940	940
Mitsubishi	Nakajima	Nakajima	Nakajima	Sasebo	Sasebo	Hitachi
1942	Dec. 1941	July 1942	Dec.1942	Jan.1943	Feb.1943	May 1944
2[††]	4	107	220	2	236	272